COMPUTERS, JOBS, AND SKILLS

The Industrial Relations of Technological Change

APPROACHES TO INFORMATION TECHNOLOGY

Series Editor
Thomas F. Carbery, *Strathclyde Business School*
University of Strathclyde
Glasgow, Scotland

Computers, Jobs, and Skills: The Industrial Relations of
   Technological Change
Christopher Baldry

Foundations of Business Information Systems
Andrew Doswell

Foundations of Business Telecommunications Management
Kenneth C. Grover

Humanizing Technology: Computers in Community Use and
   Adult Education
Elisabeth Gerver

COMPUTERS, JOBS, AND SKILLS

The Industrial Relations of Technological Change

CHRISTOPHER BALDRY

University of Strathclyde
Glasgow, Scotland

PLENUM PRESS • NEW YORK AND LONDON

Library of Congress Cataloging in Publication Data

Baldry, Christopher.
  Computers, jobs, and skills: the industrial relations of technological change /
Christopher Baldry.
      p.   cm. —(Approaches to information technology)
  Bibliography: p.
  Includes index.
  ISBN 0-306-42963-2
  1. Labor supply—Effect of technological innovations on. 2. Industrial relations—
Effect of technological innovations on. 3. Computer—Social aspects. I. Title. II.
Series.
HD6331.B245   1988   88-23384
331.11—dc19   CIP

© 1988 Plenum Press, New York
A Division of Plenum Publishing Corporation
233 Spring Street, New York, N.Y. 10013

Printed in the United States of America

FOREWORD

"Faith, Hope, and Charity and the greatest of these is Charity."

"Hardware, Software, and Liveware and the greatest of these is. . ."

As information technology ceased to be the prerogative of computer scientists and electronics engineers, those of us from other disciplines had to contend with the jargon which was already in vogue. We learned to live with "hardware" and "software." We were less enthusiastic about "liveware." Polite and some impolite questioning revealed that "liveware" was a euphemism for "people." We were not amused. As one spirited participant observed, "I refused to go home and tell my children that Almighty God had made liveware in His own image and likeness."

People are too important to be known as anything but people. Moreover, it is the importance of people that is the dominating and recurring theme of this book by Christopher Baldry. He deals with virtually every aspect of the problems concerning men and women and their recourse to the equipment. This could well become the definitive work in the field.

In addition to the details of health hazards, industrial relations, new technology agreements and the like, Dr. Baldry grapples with two great underpinning issues. One of these is whether milestones in technological achievement are to be seen as equally valid and appropriate to the overlapping road of human progress, or is technological development to be seen as a process which leads to the debasement of mankind and the reduction in the status of men and women to that of robots. The other is whether the pace of technological change is something which has its own momentum, or is it within the control of human beings. In short, the first issue is whether technological change is progressive or threatening; the second is, is it inevitable and *determining*, or is it humanly made and driven and therefore *determined*.

Many writers on information technology consider hardware, software, and people in descending order of importance. It is only recently that we have come to realize that the truth lies in the reverse flow— it is people and the human problems of information technology that are the real problems. Furthermore, this trend is going to intensify. At last, as the equipment becomes genuinely user-friendly, the take-up rates are increasing and more and more people are involved. It is for these reasons that a book such as this is appropriate.

We are all indebted to Dr. Baldry for writing it and to Plenum for making it available.

Thomas F. Carbery
Strathclyde Business School
University of Strathclyde
Glasgow, Scotland

PREFACE

The increasing study of information technology cuts across the boundaries of several existing disciplines in social science and business studies. Because the necessity to understand this technology that is transforming our lives is a current need for everyone, this book is designed to be of use to a wide range of readers and can I hope be read with interest by students, adult education groups, trade unionists, and managers alike.

To this end I have started from the assumption that the reader has no prior knowledge of industrial relations or social science in general and, wherever possible, have tried to explain concepts used in the book in as straightforward language as possible; social science or business "jargon" has been kept to a minimum except where it offers a useful shorthand tool for referring to a complex phenomenon. Where a term has slipped through the net and is not explained fully, I apologize— as I do also to those who already have a grounding in some of the areas covered and to whom I willingly risk stating the seemingly obvious.

Any technologists reading the book will soon realize that my technical background is pretty limited. To the charge that I have oversimplified some complex technological process, I can only plead that I have tried to describe it as seen by those on the receiving end: the workers and managers who have to live with the technologists' magic boxes and make them work.

Christopher Baldry

Glasgow, Scotland

ACKNOWLEDGMENTS

The author and publisher would like to thank Methuen London, Gower Publishing, New Internationalist Publications and "Radical America," Mike Cooley and Langley Technical Services, the Association of Professional Clerical and Computer Staff, and the Trades Union Congress for permission to reprint material from their publications, full details of which are cited in the references. The extract from "Computer Technology and Employment" is reprinted by permission of the National Computing Centre Limited. Thanks to Professor John Gennard for permission to use the diagram in Figure 7.

Other people have contributed directly to the production of this book. I would like to thank Debbie Campbell for her speed and efficiency in word-processing the manuscript; it is clear that new technology does not de-skill everyone! Thanks also to Terry and Rita for typing earlier drafts. Many thanks to Ed Quelch for translating my simple diagrams into such excellent graphics, and to Professor Tom Carbery and Ken Derham of Plenum for their patience and fortitude.

My colleagues at Strathclyde have contributed many ideas and criticisms during discussions of the issues, although they will all find something in this book to disagree with.

Last, thanks to Heather for everything else.

CONTENTS

LIST OF ABBREVIATIONS

TECHNICAL

CAD	Computer-aided design, or computer-aided drafting
CAM	Computer-aided manufacture
CNC	Computer-numerically controlled
DP	Data processing
EFT	Electronic funds transfer
EPOST	Electronic point of sale terminal
NC	Numerically controlled
VDU/VDT	Visual display unit/Visual display terminal

TRADE UNIONS AND TRADE UNION FEDERATIONS (WITH COUNTRY OF ORIGIN)

AFL/CIO	American Federation of Labor/Congress of Industrial Organizations (United States of America)

APEX	Association of Professional, Executive, Clerical and Computer Staff (United Kingdom)
ASTMS	Association of Scientific, Technical and Managerial Staffs (United Kingdom)
*AUEW**	Amalgamated Union of Engineering Workers (United Kingdom)
AUEW/ES	AUEW/Engineering Section (United Kingdom)
*AUEW/TASS**	AUEW/Technical, Administrative and Supervisory Section (United Kingdom)
BIFU	Banking, Insurance and Finance Union (United Kingdom)
CUPW	Canadian Union of Postal Workers (Canada)
Denki Roren	Federation of Electrical Machine workers Unions (Japan)
DGB	Deutsche Gewerkschaftsbund: German Trade Union Federation (Federal Republic of Germany)
EETPTU	Electrical, Electronic, Telecommunication and Plumbing Union (United Kingdom)
LO	Landsorganisationen i Sverige: Swedish Confederation of Trade Unions (Sweden)
MSF	Manufacturing, Science & Finance Union (United Kingdom)
NALGO	National and Local Government Officers Association (United Kingdom)
NGA	National Graphical Association (United Kingdom)
SOGAT	Society of Graphical and Allied Trades (United Kingdom)

---

* Following prolonged disagreements over policy, the British technical union TASS left the federal structure of the AUEW in 1986. Subsequently, the AUEW renamed itself the Amalgamated Engineering Union (AEU), and TASS merged in 1987 with the other major union for scientific and technical workers, ASTMS, to form MSF (see above).

| *TCO* | Tjanstemmannens centralorganisationen: Central organization of salaried employees (Sweden) |
| *TUC* | Trades Union Congress (United Kingdom) |

EMPLOYERS' ASSOCIATIONS

BDA	German Employers Federation
CBI	Confederation of British Industry
NAF	Norwegian Employers Federation
SAF	Swedish Employers Federation

OTHER LABOR RELATIONS ABBREVIATIONS

ETUI	European Trade Union Institute
ILO	International Labor Organisation
NTA	New technology agreement

COMPUTERS, JOBS, AND SKILLS

PROLOGUE

In the word-processing pool it is 11:00 AM. The operator adjusts her headphones and keys in the next piece of work from the invisible bank of taped dictation. The screen cursor moves to the starting position for the standard format for this type of document, ensuring that it will in every way be identical to similar documents produced by her colleagues. Numbers in the top corner of the screen denote her code number, the time, and tell her that it is the sixth piece of work she has started that morning. There is no indication of how many more items are reposing in the tape bank. She pauses for a moment and gratefully takes the cup of sweetened coffee from the adjacent cart. She glances around. All the other operators' eyes are glued to their screens, their fingers quietly pattering the keys in the subdued lighting of the office. Swiftly but deliberately she pours coffee over the high-tech keyboard. The screen goes blank.

1

INTRODUCTION

*I submit to the public a small machine of my own invention, by means
of which you alone may, without any effort, perform all the operations
of arithmetic and may be relieved of the work which so often fatigued
your spirit when you worked with the counters and the pen.*

Blaise Pascal, 1642

A TRANSFORMING TECHNOLOGY

Unless he or she has spent the last 10 years in the depths of the equa-
torial rain forests or a cave in the Himalayas, the average citizen of
any of the major industrial societies cannot have failed to be aware
that the advent of microelectronics and computerization has begun to
profoundly affect our lives both at work and at home.

It is probably true to say that never before has a single technological development been simultaneously introduced into such a wide
range of social and economic activities. In our homes we are already
used to a modest range of new products based in microprocessors—
digital watches, calculators, video games, and home computers—but
in the workplace, where undoubtedly the greatest changes have so far
taken place, shopfloor workers are witnessing the increasing use of
robotics for repetitive jobs such as spot welding or paint spraying, the
spread of computerized warehousing and inventories, computer numerically controlled (CNC) machine tools, computerized monitoring
and output control in process industries, and computer testing of quality control in general.

In the office, designers and technicians are making the transition to computer-aided design (CAD), typists to using word-processors, and white-collar and managerial staff of all grades are increasingly likely to use a variety of desktop computers, accounting machines, and mainframe terminals (even if these are occasionally disguised as "executive workstations"). Electronic communications have exalted the humble telephone by augmenting it with fully electronic switchboards, the use of optical fibers and satellites, and connecting it to facsimile transmission and viewdata systems.

In the service sector, "people-to-people" services, previously untouched by technological change, are being transformed, as epitomized by the first moves toward cashless shopping and electronic banking transactions.

In response to these developments, newspapers, magazines, and journals during the early 1980s regularly ran articles (usually with titles that referred to chips being "down" or "with everything") that either pointed to yet another new and ingenious use of the new technology (as it is still being called for convenience, although the basic elements of it are by now relatively old), showed how a problem of administration had been overcome by computerization, chronicled the struggles of a group of workers whose jobs were threatened by some productive innovation, described how disabled people had been offered new opportunities to communicate through touch-sensitive keyboards, or stressed the need for our childrens' education to include "computer literacy."

Toward a Brave New World?

Many of these articles or television documentaries, however, have subsequently gone much further, moving from mere description to social prediction, and have spoken of the microelectronic or information revolution as being an event or process at least as historically momentous as the first industrial revolution.

Just as the industrial revolution shifted the type of society from agricultural-rural to industrial-urban, so, it is claimed, the new technology will usher in a new type of society, the details of which are as yet unclear but in which it is usually alleged that paid work will not only be generally easier and more personally fulfilling but will also take up a smaller proportion of our lives. Now these are fairly sweeping statements. It is one thing for us, as managers, shopfloor workers, technical staff, teachers, or nurses, to try to come to terms with and adjust to new ways of working, but quite another thing to be told that the very concepts *work* or *leisure* may be becoming historically obsolete. It will therefore be necessary in a book whose focus is the interaction of the "new technology" with the world of work, to cover both of these aspects of the current technical changes—their impact on our working lives now, and what is predicted to be their long-term impact on the role of work in the wider society.

This is not as simple as at first it might seem. We are already aware that attitudes of different groups of people toward the new technology can be diametrically opposed: some are for as much of it as possible as quickly as possible, others dead set against it. This suggests that simple description is not enough. Whereas it has a limited usefulness in that we may need to recognize a CAD workstation or a CNC milling machine if we come across one, we also need to go beyond "gee-whiz" accounts of the latest developments if we are to *understand* the nature of the technical change that is going on around us and the reactions to it of different groups in society, including our own.

ATTITUDES AND PHOBIAS

In seeking to analyze the interaction between man or woman and machine or, on a macro level, between technology and society, we almost immediately come up against powerful values and attitudes toward technology in general which pervade the cultures of all the industrial societies and which, awkwardly, are not always consistent.

We can drastically simplify the complexity of these cultural views of technology by treating them in terms of two sets of opposites. The first pair of opposites concerns whether technology is viewed either as an index of human progress or conversely as something which threatens to reduce our full human potential to something closer to that of the machine itself.

Technology as Progress

The *technology-as-progress* view is currently reflected in the assertions that microelectronic technology will be in some way liberating:

it will free us from soul-destroying or physically unpleasant tasks (already for example, simple repetitive assembly and paint-spraying can be done by robots), and the sheer improved productivity of the technology will free us from the necessity of working for so much of our lives, offering us more time for leisure and creativity.

We can almost call this the "official" view of new technology as it is rooted in attitudes toward technology and the application of science that have provided the basis for industrial society's understanding and transformation of its environment of several hundred years. Since the intellectual and ideological struggles of the Renaissance in Europe, we have been taught how science liberated us from the restrictions of medieval religious interpretations of our world, enabling us to understand and hence—in crucial (if limited) ways—to control and transform our physical and social environment and its resources. The cumulative understanding that we call science underpins industrialism: the laws of mechanics and gases become incorporated into the steam engine.

Similarly, we know that the application of science to social problems has cured disease and lengthened our life expectancy and the chances of our children growing to adulthood; the pressures on food supply that these developments represented were solved, in the industrial societies at least, partly by the application of science to agriculture, with corresponding increases in crop yields and productivity.

There is a pervading tendency therefore to regard scientific and technological developments as inevitably progressive and on the whole a good thing. Technological development in this view becomes synonymous with social progress—proof that we are getting on top of our problems.

Critical Approaches to Technology

Parallel to the development of this view, there developed its antithesis, a critique of the uses to which technology has been put, which runs through the work of the early industrial critics such as Ruskin, Morris, and Marx, and which today points out that many obvious problems exist in the world to which we are not directing our scientific resources. Instead, as this view asserts, we have developed even more technologically sophisticated ways of killing each other, to the point where we now have the capacity to destroy the whole planet.

This critique points to the fact that technological development has regularly stripped men and women of their employment, often the only jobs which they have known or had experience of, tossing them into the ebb and flow of the labor market. Even where jobs remain, one of the dominant themes of this critique—not so much of technology *per se* but of the forms into which industrial technology has been developed and the uses to which it has been put—is that far from enriching our lives, it has in several crucial ways been a dehumanizing process, taking away from men and women aspects of themselves such as skill, creativity, and the ability to control their own work. The technology seems either to make people redundant or makes redundant important aspects of their humanity.

This idea has had a very real resurgence with the advent of computerization. We had become gradually accustomed to the replacement of human physical activity by machines so that in the popular imagination mechanization went hand in hand with industrialization. Then when human guidance and control was replaced mechanically to produce the phenomenon of "automation," there was a new period of concern and mental adjustment, and finally from the 1940s onward computers offered us the prospect of genuine "thinking machines" and thus the replacement of that final element that seemed to distinguish us as human beings—mental activity.

These developments were seized by science fiction writers, futurologists, and assorted crystal-ball gazers to produce an image of the future dominated by legions of robots or controlled by all-seeing, all-knowing computers. This theme of "the machines taking over" seems to have struck a responsive chord in the public mind, and certainly in the early stages of computerization, when the average member of the public's only contact with computers was the necessity to deal with some anonymous mainframe in another part of the country in order to pay his phone bill or renew her driving license, there was a good deal of suspicion of computers in general, based on the fact that most people seem to like to conduct transactions with other people rather than with machines. Although some of this general suspicion has abated with increased familiarity with the technology, nevertheless when the employee is informed that he or she will in future be using a piece of computerized technology to help with the work, this is still likely to raise the nagging question of who will be helping whom: will the new technology be a tool to facilitate the job and remove elements of drudgery, or will the worker be transformed into a machine-minder, simply keeping the beast regularly fed and watered with data and information? These issues are examined more fully in Chapter 3.

Determined or Determining?

This first set of opposing attitudes toward technology that sees it as representing either social progress or a dehumanizing tendency is closely related to the second set of opposites, which hinge around the degree to which such technological developments should be seen as inevitable or as subject to human control.

The differences in the ways in which these two approaches are likely to view information technology can paradoxically best be illustrated by the way they view the causal processes within the first industrial revolution.

We have already mentioned the prediction that microelectronic technology will usher in a new type of "information society" just as the industrial revolution is commonly said to have produced industrial society. The force for change in this model is identified in both cases as being the technology itself—the steam engine or the microchip. In this view, the technology, once developed, has a series of "impacts" whether we like it or not. Because we have been told that science develops cumulatively, the assumption is that scientific discoveries must be applied as part of the process of advancing our knowledge of our environment and our capacity to alter it, and, once applied, these applications will inevitably change our lives. The steam engine, it is argued, because of its ability to drive several textile machines at the same time, required lots of people to work together under one roof rather than individually in their own homes as they had done with hand manufacture. Also, because of its high cost, this new technology could no longer be owned by the weaver or spinner but only by the entrepreneur with the necessary capital to invest. Hence the application of scientific knowledge to the development of the steam engine seems to bring about the social and organizational relationships which typify early industrialism: The separation of work and home, the development of the factory, and the creation of a capital-less working class selling its labor to the owners of the capital.

It can be seen that this model of societal change is likely to lead the holder to accord to any widely applicable new technology, such as microelectronics, the power to transform social organization both in the workplace and perhaps in the wider society also.

The counterpoint of this view criticizes it as viewing history in terms of "technological determinism," and in reply argues that it is not machines that make history or change societies, but rather the decisions of people acting separately or, more usually, collectively. It is people that develop and make the machines and the techniques, and they choose to develop technologies to solve certain problems but not others, depending on the dominant priorities of the day.

The earliest industrial innovations benefited the home textile worker and the factory owner alike, but it was the desire to increase profitability that made the early entrepreneurs seek to develop factory work and factory discipline rather than continuing to rely on the old putting-out system. The gradual development of industrial work relations and the factory preceded the widespread use of the steam engine by some decades,[1] but once the factory became the dominant form of productive organization, then it also became the framework within which future technological developments were likely to take place.

In other words, the priorities of the age steered the direction of applied science. So today, critics of industrial technology point out that science is seldom directed toward solving all existing technical problems (e.g., world hunger, or keeping old-age pensioners warm during the winter) but usually only particular ones (such as the productivity of the existing "have" nations, or the arms race), whereas its supporters can point to labor-saving devices in the home and a constantly rising standard of living.

CHARACTERISTICS OF INFORMATION TECHNOLOGY

To recap the theme of the book, we can say that in understanding the reactions of groups in society to technological change, we have to take into account deep-rooted attitudes that see technology as:

1. *Either* progressive *or* threatening, and
2. *Either* inevitable and determining, *or* a human creation and therefore determinable.

These themes recur throughout the book often in the most unlikely places.

What we have said about these conflicting sets of attitudes could apply to any area of technical change. In order to more fully understand how microelectronics in particular is affecting our lives and whether it is something more than just another clever idea, we need now to examine the unique features of new technology.

A report by the British Advisory Council for Applied Research and Development (ACARD)[2] in the late 1970s identified microelectronics and computers as the most influential technology of this century and pinpointed several major characteristics:

1. *It extends and displaces a wide range of intellectual or instructive skills.* As we noted earlier, only recently has the mechanization of mental effort become a reality. Early attempts were, not surprisingly, mechanical in their operation; adding and calculating machines were devised by mathemeticians and philosophers such as Pascal and Leibniz in the seventeenth century, and Babbage in the nineteenth century, and the idea of storing complicated sequences of instructions to machines or large volumes of data on punched cards was the basis of the Jacquard loom and the Hollerith card reader. However, it was not until the development of electricity and the science of electronics that it became rapidly possible to transfer information at speeds much closer to that of the human brain, and to store such information in prodigious quantities.

2. *It is all-pervasive.* Computers are designed to handle information, and the communication and exchange of information (by which we mean not simply facts, but also ideas, values, and concepts) is a common feature of virtually all our social activity, whether we are working, shopping or enjoying ourselves. Thus the potential range of computer applications is vast. Also, because they handle information rather than simply reproduce actions, computers possess two other characteristics. First, their use is not confined by their physical location. Mainframes can drive terminals many miles away, and the material originating on a keyboard at one end of the country can chatter off a printer at the other. This points to the second of these characteristics, that computers and computer-based systems have the capacity to be mutually interactive, or, to put it simply (and anthropomorphically), they can be made to speak to each other. It is these two characteristics which have given rise to predictions of radical changes in organizational structure and the more far-reaching predictions of the electronic information society.

3. *It is still advancing rapidly.* Microelectronics and computers can be said to have undertaken an extremely successful colonization of existing and hitherto separate technologies. This is nowhere more clearly visible than in the modern office where office staff, instead of operating the traditional variety of devices—typewriters, copiers, calculators, telephones—each engineered for a specific purpose, increasingly use multifunctional "information technology." A keyboard can

now act as a typewriter, calculator, desk diary, initiator of electronic mail, or source of access to electronic filing.

4. *It is very cheap and getting cheaper*. The early computers were huge and expensive. They had to be housed in special air-conditioned shrines and could only be talked to by an elite of white-coated high priests who alone knew the sacred language. As long as these conditions held, only the really large corporations could become computerized. Today the small shopkeeper can work out his tax returns on a computer so small he can keep it in his desk drawer and so cheap that he can buy it in a chain store. A microprocessor chip, which by the early 1980s cost as little as $20.00, had the computing power of the first commercial IBM machine, which in the 1950s would have set a corporation back some $1 million, and it has been estimated that since 1960 the cost of computation has dropped 100,000-fold.[3]

In addition to these major characteristics, the ACARD report added the prediction that the technology will become abundantly available from international sources, thus giving no one nation a head start through its possession of some scarce resource (although, as we shall see in the next chapter, the real structure of the international microelectronics industry often works against this). Last, the report points out that the technology has an exceptionally high level of reliability.

Summing up these features, Jenkins and Sherman (1979) conclude that the technology is analogous to earlier transforming techniques such as the steam engine and the electric motor, both of which were capable of adaption and use in a wide variety of contexts.[4] In addition, they see computers as having specific abilities to modify existing production and service processes. They can respond faster than human reaction times, they can work in environments hostile to human health, and they can diagnose problems (such as the cause of mechanical breakdown) providing these fall within a predetermined range of options.

TECHNOLOGY AS THE MIDWIFE OF SOCIAL CHANGE

As we have already remarked, the industrial revolution was revolutionary in the sense that the whole structure of society shifted, new social classes emerged, new work relationships were formed based on a monetary contract rather than feudal obligation, work was separated from the home with new social values and attitudes toward work and nonwork, and a landless working population was crowded from the countryside into mushrooming towns and cities.

Therefore, in attempting to discern the long-term implications for patterns of work in our society, we have to ask whether the sort of characteristics noted in the previous pages make the new information technology so different from previous innovations that we have to see it as heralding a new transformation of society. Or conversely, is it simply the latest episode in the long story of industrialization, just another generation of clever machines?

We will return to this theme more fully in Chapter 6, but we can say that if a similar degree of social change is commencing, then its transitional effects may well be visible more immediately than were those of the first industrial revolution, which, despite its popular label, was in Britain a fairly protracted affair affecting only some sectors of the economy at any one time.

Compared to this slow and uneven rate of development, computerization has the potential, as we have seen, to be adopted in the industrial societies at a very fast rate. Semiconductors were first developed in the early 1950s, the first single-chip integrated circuit appeared as recently as 1963, and products containing far more developed forms of this technology were installed and working in our homes and workplaces by the late 1970s.

It might be said that these differences are simply the result of historical development, that we should not expect history to repeat itself and that any future social transformation will in all likelihood be more rapid than previous ones. But if this is the case, there could be additional cause for concern, given another major difference between the current computer revolution and the first industrial revolution. In the early nineteenth century, technological innovation took place within an expanding economy despite which a well-chronicled degree of misery and deprivation was experienced by large groups of people. In contrast, microelectronics have been taken up at a time of recurrent economic crisis when unemployment in the industrial societies is still numbered in tens of millions. Jenkins and Sherman make the point that, in this climate of slow growth, investment in the new technology is being undertaken not to produce new products or new materials but rather to increase the efficiency of existing systems of production, resulting in increasingly capital-intensive economics. We examine the implications of this for the aggregate level of employment in Chapter 2.

The Problems of Change—A Note about the Rest of the Book

This brief overview of some of the peculiarities of the new technology points us toward some of the problem areas in the changing workplace that are the theme of this book.

The historical experience of technological change has been that a new technology invariably supplants and replaces existing skills and tasks. Whereas these have in the past been mainly physical skills (the prior separation of mental and physical labor is dealt with more fully in Chapter 3), computerization represents the automation of mental work. Several questions arise from this: will new jobs be created to replace those that the technology makes redundant? Will new skills be required or will those jobs that are left be less meaningful than previously? How will these jobs be rewarded? Are there any new hazards associated with the technology that workers should be aware of?

The ability of electronic information to transcend the boundaries of the office or factory may mean that the structure of our workplaces may undergo profound changes: both the organizational structure (will there still be the necessity for hierarchical bureaucratic management structures?) and the physical structure with perhaps a great deal more decentralization and fewer of the massive concentrations of labor power under one roof that we associated with heavy industry. This latter development may even, it has been suggested, break down the home–work distinction, as already several software and insurance firms have started to utilize this aspect of information technology to experiment with home working for their staff.

If the applicability and cheapness of the technology does lead to a widespread and rapid rate of take-up, this itself could be problematic for the economy as a whole: can all sections of the economy take the strain of simultaneous adjustment?

Although perhaps such wider issues could be regarded as the concern of politicians, the day-to-day problems of adjusting to change have to be thrashed out between management and its workforce. A final question here, and an important one, is whether management and unions have the resources or the knowledge to cope adequately with the scale of change. Are the traditional structures of collective bargaining, with their emphasis on reform within the status quo, best equipped either to give the unions' members adequate protection against some of the newer issues involved or to ensure management's adaptation to changed organizational principles?

The core of the book is an understanding of the industrial relations of technical change, an explanation of why and how new technology can present different sets of problems to different groups in the workplace and the various ways in which those problems can be tackled, if not entirely resolved (Chapters 4 and 5). In the course of this explanation, I have stepped outside of the boundaries of industrial relations as conventionally defined, partly for the reasons suggested above, partly to do justice to the fact that many of the issues at stake are more complex than they first seem, and partly because—as we shall see—new technology is just one of several developments that may make many of our current industrial relations practices and structures historically obsolete.

The reference and source materials that I have used, and that are found in the Bibliography, range from those works that are readily available to most library users in Europe and North America to the fairly obscure (and sometimes short-lived) pamphlet or article. I make no apologies for the latter, which are used for three good reasons. First, it is not surprising that much of the material on information technology in the workplace has been produced by those on the receiving end of change—employees and their trade unions. I have thus drawn quite heavily on a wide variety of trade-union publications for concrete examples of the problems of change.

Second, it is clear from the preliminary remarks in this chapter that information technology is being used to change the structure and nature of work not just in a single industry or even a single country, but in all the industrial nations. Thus, I have tried to draw together corroborative material from different industrial societies; some of this material, especially that in translation, has been gleaned from some unlikely sources.

The final reason is that the author of any work on a swiftly evolving technology faces the risk of almost instant obsolescence. There are probably several statements in this book which have already been superceded by events by the time that you read this: here the pamphlet and the article have the advantage over the book of drawing our attention to developments in a more immediate way.

I hope therefore that this will prove to be a challenging book. It is above all critical of those ready-made formulas for change which dismiss the fears and apprehensions of ordinary people as pseudo-problems standing in the way of progress. It also contains criticisms both of the trade unions for a frequent narrowness of vision and of management for tending to assess systems purely on technical or eco-

nomic criteria to the detriment of the social and organizational consequences.

Computers, Jobs, and Skills offers no instant panaceas to the problems of adjusting to new technology, advocating neither an uncritical
open-arms welcome to new technology as the answer to all our problems, nor a total rejection of the computer and all its works. Instead,
the theme throughout is that there is little that is inevitable about the
consequences of technological innovation, but that human choice is a
constant factor at every stage of the process. What then becomes problematic is who makes the choices and what are their priorities.

It is hoped that by pricking the balloon of the more fashionable
myths and putting the issues in a wider context, this discussion may
contribute both to more fruitful analysis, and to practice more firmly
rooted in understanding.

DISCUSSION QUESTIONS

1. Are the different and conflicting social attitudes toward technology simply
   mindless prejudices, or are they based on historical experience?
2. In what ways does information technology differ from previous generations
   of automated equipment, and how might such differences prove significant
   for the organization of work?

REFERENCES

1. Kumar, *Prophecy and progress: The sociology of industrial and post-industrial society,* Penguin, Harmondsworth (1978), pp. 325–326.
2. Advisory Council for Applied Research and Development, *Technological change:
   Threats and opportunities for the United Kingdom,* Her Majesty's Stationery Office,
   London (1979).
3. A. Perlowski, The smart machine revolution, in: T. Forester (ed.), *The Microelectronics Revolution* (T. Forester, ed.), Blackwell, Oxford (1980), pp. 105–124.
4. C. Jenkins & B. Sherman, *The collapse of work,* Eyre Methuen, London (1979), pp.
   60–61.

2

EMPLOYMENT

The demand for commodities is not the demand for labour.
John Stuart Mill

TECHNOLOGY AND EMPLOYMENT

To say that technology affects employment seems almost a truism: as citizens of an industrial society, we intuitively expect technological changes to manifest themselves in movements both of the number of people employed and in the types of jobs that they do and the skills that these require. This is, of course, an expectation peculiar to our own historical era, the era of industrialism, which brought with it the social institution of an everchanging labor market. It is here that most of us endeavor to sell our only source of economic livelihood—our ability to work, whether by hand or brain. To do this we have to keep aware of what skills and trades are marketable and which ones are no longer in demand, and changes in technology run as an inevitable thread through these calculations.

In a preindustrial subsistence economy, such as that of medieval Europe, the connection between technology and employment was far less obvious. Tasks were allocated by other means than the market, for example, through inherited obligation, the cycle of the seasons, or the vagaries of the climate. The technology, the methods of agriculture and of transport, remained relatively unchanging. For most people it was a given, unvariable factor, part of the scenery and not something to react to.

By contrast, the last two hundred years have seen, on the one hand, the relentless application of science to the business of transforming raw materials into commodities, resulting in a stream of technological developments that continue to change our lives and lifestyles; on the other hand, an apparent constantly shifting demand for labor and for specific skills and attributes in the labor force that have within single generations resulted in acute swings from periods of full employment to periods of mass worklessness.

In their analyses of unemployment, economists have traditionally differentiated between frictional and structural unemployment. Short-term *frictional* unemployment is defined as the gap between leaving one job and taking up another, and is treated as being inevitable in any society with a mobile labor market. Beveridge, one of the architects of British postwar economic policies, defined *full employment* at the level of 3% unemployment or less; 100% employment was seen as "over-full" employment, which would lead to unwelcome rigidities in the labor market.

Structural unemployment is seen as longer term and as the consequence of older industries declining in importance and demand, and newer industries not yet being sufficiently established to take up the slack, in other words, the signs of an economy restructuring itself, almost invariably as the concomitant of some process of technological change.

There are however some difficulties in using these labels as a basis for understanding the technology–employment relationship. The very notion of frictional unemployment assumes the normal state of affairs to be full employment. More realistically, in economic circumstances like the present, what starts out as a short-term frictional state, may soon develop into a contribution to long-term restructuring. The latter concept, of structural unemployment, has a similar equilibrium assumption built into it, the assumption that eventually a new industry *will* arise to replace the old and its demand for labor.

The Example of History

Superficially, the history of industrialism would seem to lend support to this assumption. The industrial revolution in Britain was preceded by the transformation of agriculture, providing the surplus labor out of which was formed the new industrial working class. In turn, the decline in demand for the skills of groups like the handloom weavers was matched by an increase in demand for other trades.

It is easy to draw comfort from this apparent continued ability of industrial society to conceive new technical and economic activities, and to see a causal relationship between technical change and economic growth, where one is essential for the other. If, as a result of technical improvement, goods and services are produced more cheaply, it is argued, resources will be released that will then be available for mobilization to provide further employment. Examples of this argument can be found in some of the early attempts to look at the social effects of microelectronics. The British government-backed think tank, the Central Policy Review Staff (CPRS), in 1978 noted that, historically, technical change had been a source of economic growth, and concluded with satisfaction that "This should be equally true of microelectronics."[1]

This is too simple a model, however, because it first assumes a closed economic system, whereas in today's global economy, the surplus value created by technical advance in one society may well be "mobilized" elsewhere on the planet. It is certainly too simple a view of history, implying as it does a harmonious and continuous transition from one stage of technological development to the next.

In reality, we know that the important technological shifts within industrial societies have been accompanied by severe social dislocation. The shift from agriculture to industrial employment already cited, was accompanied by mass emiseration and appalling social conditions in the mushrooming towns of early industrial Europe. This early period of industrialism brought forth great outbursts of popular protest such as the Luddite movement in Britain, similar machine-breaking waves in France and Germany, the Chartists, the Paris Commune, and the European revolts of 1848.

This underlines the point that for the economist, although, frictional and/or structural unemployment may represent "released" resources, the people themselves seldom feel "released." The ending of a previous way of earning one's living is often a massive personal and collective crisis.

Furthermore, these periods of social crisis have not been confined to the early years of industrialism. The whole history of our societies has been marked by periodic booms and slumps, which many have tried to connect with cycles of technical development.

There has of late been a resurgence of interest in the theories of the 1920s Soviet economist Kondratiev and his model of the "long wave" or 50-year cycle.[2] Kondratiev (before his enforced disappearance in the direction of a Stalinist labor camp) studied historical patterns of capitalist investment and concluded that at the beginning of each long wave there is an increase in output and productivity associated with the spread of a technical innovation. This increase eventually plateaus and lasts approximately 25 years. The plateau is followed by a downturn into 25-year depression associated with a decline in the fortunes of the previous generation of technology. On the downward curve of the wave, there is a search for some technological improvement that will increase productivity and profitability, and this provides the basis for the next upturn of the cycle.

Attempts to identify these waves historically have tended to flounder, depending on which particular industrial society is taken for the model. For Britain, the first wave is usually taken to be the period 1780–1840, associated with the steam engine, the next wave of 1840–1890 being associated with the railway engine and the electric motor. Today, it is argued, the boom industry of the 1940s and 1950s, the automobile industry, is declining but the seeds of the next boom are to be discerned in the nascent microelectronics industry.

Although perhaps lacking in precise historical validity, the model does have the advantage of suggesting that technological development has tended to be discontinuous and cyclical rather than the unilinear smooth harmonious affair that terms like *progress, advance* and *development* tend to suggest, and that it has led in the past to pronounced social tensions and crises. With this in mind, we now have to examine the most useful way of treating the relationship between technology and employment.

Impacts and Processes

Wilkinson has pointed out that there are two major approaches to analyzing this relationship.[3] The first, and most commonly encountered, view is that technology is a neutral force arising out of an idea or invention, which is applied for purely economic reasons and has a consequent *impact*, which may be for good or ill. The second assumption treats the use of technology as a process which involves and expresses choices, priorities, and power relationships in the wider society.

Because the majority of studies so far have been based on the first assumption, we first examine what the impact and effects of new technology on employment are supposed to be; we then look at the evidence for microelectronics thus far and attempt to discern if any of these effects are actually taking place, and finally we return to the second assumption, to see if it contributes a more useful explanatory perspective.

The first way in which any new technology affects employment depends on whether the innovations are used for new products and processes, or whether they represent a replacement technology in the production of existing goods and services.

New products can have a positive effect on employment levels in two ways: first, by requiring people to make them, and second, by stimulating demand in the economy and thus generally helping to raise the level of economic activity. However, new products can have a negative effect on employment, by causing a withering away of demand for existing products as people switch from one to another.

The effects of using new technology to lower the costs of production of an *existing* product very much depend on the state of the market. In an unsaturated or expanding market (e.g., the early nineteenth-century cotton industry), the ability to lower the price of the product will stimulate demand and expand employment by making the product more widely available to the mass of the population. In a saturated market, however, in which there is a fierce competition among producers for market share (e.g., the late-twentieth-century automobile industry), using new technology to lower costs is more likely to result in higher productivity for an unchanging labor force, or in actual job reductions. Against this argument, it could be demonstrated that rising costs and low competitiveness leads to jobs being lost anyway and that the increased productivity may enable the company to increase the range of services it offers.

On a macro level, supply-side economists argue that even if jobs are lost in the short term, the subsequent lowering of the price of labor stimulates economic activity, that is, the "release" of resources.

When technological change does displace labor from a given location, the degree to which this change affects macro employment levels is said to depend on a number of factors:

1. Demographic and labor-market movements that may be oc-

curring at the time of innovation (e.g., the increase in the proportion of women entering the labor market).

2. The scope of the new technology—the number of different applications and therefore employment sectors it is capable of being used in. The most far-reaching innovations of the past, such as the steam engine and the electric motor, could be used in a wide range of applications across the employment spectrum.

3. The rate of diffusion—the speed at which the new technology is taken up.

These variables could apply to *all* instances of technological change. To be more specific, let us look at microelectronics and computers in terms of their specific characteristics that may mark them off from previous technological artifacts.

Replacement and Displacement

Understandably, many of the initial expectations about the effects of computers on employment were based on earlier experiences of automation. There are, however, important differences. The first phase of automation, so-called "hard" automation, consisted of the replacement of human physical activity by mechanical means. This was followed by an intermediate stage of "soft" automation, epitomized by numerically controlled (N/C) machine tools, whereby most of the mental processes that controlled the machining were removed from being the responsibility of the machinist and lodged in a control program; (sometimes this difference is referred to as the difference between mechanization and automation proper). We return to the significance of this difference in Chapter 3, but here we simply note that it was a precursor to the current application of computers, which now offers the potential replacement of human mental activity.

The difference between hard automation and computerization, the difference between concrete and abstract action, is reflected in different effects on employment that we might usefully designate as *replacement effects* and *displacement effects*. A robot, for example, is essentially the application of the programmable qualities of a computer to existing principles of automation, and it has a concrete replacement effect on employment. A robot spot welder or spray painter replaces several human welders or painters, owing to its greater productivity (no tea breaks, lunch hours, or toilet breaks) and its ability to work round the clock (where the human job would be split between two or three individuals working consecutive shifts). The robot is doing the same job as the humans used to do, in the same location. Thus at Austin Rover's modernized Longbridge factory, 50 employees plus robots now do car-assembly work previously done by 220 employees.

Computerization seldom works as straightforwardly as this. Consider a small typing office where the typewriters are replaced by word processors. It may be that all the secretaries get retrained to be word-processor operators, and it appears that new technology has resulted in no job loss. This is true in the location where the equipment is operating; but the typewriter represented a single moment in the information flow. Once a document was typed someone else had to mail it to its destination, someone else to file it, and so on. Word processors, when integrated into office systems, significantly capture many of these functions. The material is filed electronically on disk, or sent downline to a printer (perhaps in another location) at the touch of a key. So, despite appearances in the actual typing office, there may well be downstream displacement effects on employment, which are experienced in the mailing room, the filing room, and so on.

This represents a significant challenge for trade unions trying to protect their members' jobs. In the first place, it is much harder to attribute cause and effect by asserting that specific items of new technology are directly responsible for particular instances of job loss. Secondly, in multiunion workplaces (such as in Britain), the jobs lost may be covered by a different union from that which organizes the employees actually operating the equipment. It may be that one is a manual (blue collar) union, the other clerical.

Whereas computerized equipment clearly has the potential to both replace and displace some jobs, it has been argued that new jobs and tasks will be created by the introduction of new technology, so that on balance there may be no net job loss. The CPRS report quoted earlier, gave the example of the introduction of early generation computers into the British Civil Service in the 1960s, which it claimed did not result in the widespread job loss predicted at the time, but actually led to some job expansion.[4]

This, however, cannot be taken as a reliable guide. It refers to the era of centralized data-processing, where the new systems did indeed create a demand for key-punch operators, programmers, and other new occupations. The difference compared to today is that these early mainframes existed in splendid isolation—they were in a different technical universe from the telephone system, the typing pool, and the photo-copier. The second distinguishing characteristic of today's generation of new technology, (and the reason why items performing different functions can all be dubbed "new technology") is, as we saw in Chapter 1, that it is interactive.

The Mechanized Information Flow

This interactive property makes possible the linking of hitherto discrete items of productive equipment into networks of electronically relayed information. This suggests that where a function in the preau-tomated information flow is performed by a specific group of employ-ees, they are likely to find themselves electronically bypassed (see the example of printing compositors examined in Chapter 4), and that if there *is* any net increase in jobs, it is more likely to occur in an early intermediate stage of technical change, before full link-up is possible.

A good example of this is offered by the history of technical de-velopments in the engineering industry. Around the 1930's, the drafts-person produced working drawings of the product in the drawing office, (often using a knowledge of engineering machining gained from a shop-floor apprenticeship), passed the drawing on to the skilled lathe or milling machine operator who, in turn, used both knowledge and ex-perience to judge the most effective way to execute the job.

In the 1960s, numerically controlled (N/C) machine tools took away much of the skilled man's responsibility and control, but in turn created a demand for people to program the machines; so new grades of part-programmers and tape-punch operators came into being, usually located in the work-study department. In the 1970s, computer-aided design (CAD) began to revolutionize the work of the drawing office, cutting the demand for certain types of drawing-office staff such as detail-draftspersons. Today, the prospect of full CAD/CAM (computer-aided design and manufacture) systems, threatens to by-pass the part-programmers, as drive-programs for computer-numerically controlled (CNC) machines will be created directly from the CAD data base in the drawing office. These changes are represented in Figure 1.

The wide applicability of microelectronics and computerization to activities that up to now have been performed on functionally separate items of equipment (typewriters, drawing boards, and lathes), and the interactive properties of the new technology, open up the possibilities

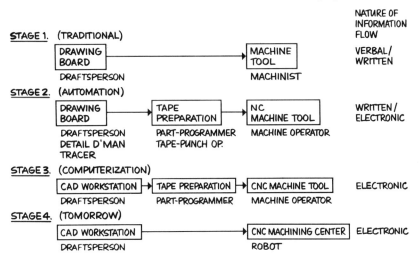

Figure 1. Technical development in engineering.

not only of single integrated systems like CAD/CAM, but whole productive systems integrating everything from design, and whole administrative systems summed up in the image of the "paperless office." Perhaps even more significantly, the interactive properties of the new technology mean that employment effects of specific systems are no longer confined to the boundaries of single organizations, or even the boundaries of given economic categories.

Figure 2 shows the sequence of developments in two hitherto discrete areas of commercial employment, retailing and banking. Until recently, we were used to going to the bank and, served by a friendly staff, withdrawing some cash, or perhaps getting a new checkbook. We then decided to go shopping, trundled the shopping cart around the store, and at the checkout watched as the mountain of goods were added up by the friendly (this is a hypothetical case you understand) checkout girl. We paid for our groceries with cash or a check. At the end of the day, the store processed all its takings in cash and checks, and banked them. The checks were then passed from the shop's bank to the customers' banks for processing—a lot of people were involved.

Increasingly, however, the customer is getting used to two new aspects of the new technology. At the bank, he or she is able to insert a plastic cash-card into a dispenser in the outside wall and complete the transaction without seeing any bank staff at all, a development that

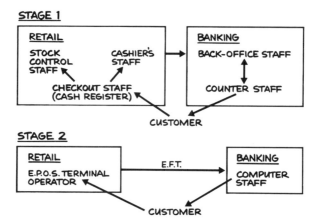

Figure 2. The employment consequences of electronically linking previously discrete economic activities.

is worrying the banking unions. At the store, the customer may find his or her goods processed by point-of-sale terminals which, by optically reading the bar-coded goods, increase the rate of customer throughput and reduce the overall demand for both checkout staff and the people that price-label the cans and packages. Such terminals also log a stock list of all produce sold, reducing the demand for stock-control personnel.

Both these developments occurred autonomously within their respective economic categories but their common basis in computerization allows the third and most significant stage, where they are linked together via Electronic Funds Transfer. Here the customer is able to insert a bank card into the store's point of sale terminal and the cost of the transaction is directly debited from the customer's account and transferred to that of the store. No money, checks, or credit cards change hands, and very few people are involved in the process. This is by no means a future development. Several supermarkets in France are experimenting with this already, and customers of a leading Scottish bank can buy their gas electronically from selected filling stations.

Computers and Employment—A Terminal Case?

The, at present latent, potential of microelectronic technology poses an obvious immediate threat to a wide range of existing jobs and occupations. Little wonder that, in the late 1970s, the first attempts to comprehensively review the implications of the new technology almost universally painted a very bleak scenario of future levels of employment in the industrialized societies.

Professor Tom Stonier, in a paper for the International Metal-workers Federation, predicted that within 30 years we would need only 10% of the current labor force to be engaged in direct manufacturing to provide us with all our material needs.[5] Barron and Curnow predicted technology-induced unemployment in Britain could reach rates of up to 15%.[6] Even in Japan, the influential Ministry for International Trade and Investment (MITI) was predicting inevitable employment problems by the mid 1980s unless the rate of economic growth picked up.[7]

Reports looking at specific sectors were even more alarming. The very thoughtful "Report to the President of France" by Nora and Minc, highlighted key service areas like insurance and banking where, they felt, employment levels would be 30% less than they would have been without computerization.[8] An unpublished but subsequently widely quoted report by the West German Siemens Company as early as 1976, concluded that 25–30% of all office jobs could become automated.[9] In the United States, the Society of Manufacturing Engineers and the University of Michigan predicted that by 1990 programable automation (robotics) could replace half the employment in the assembly of small components and half the employment in automobile final assembly.[10]

Whereas some of the studies quoted above stated that eventually new industries would compensate for technologically induced job loss, some studies were not so sure. The General Secretary of the British white-collar union the Association of Scientific, Technical, and Managerial Staff & his chief research officer went so far as to predict the "collapse of work":

> Remain as we are, reject the new technologies and we face unemployment of up to 5.5m by the end of the century. Embrace the new technologies, accept the challenge and we end up with unemployment of about 5m. . . . What is clear is that whatever road we take, work will collapse.[11]

These first spectacular doom and gloom scenarios, (or, in some cases, spectacular uses made of honest attempts to predict trends), can be subject to criticism on several points. First, the observation that an improvement to contemporary processes of production results in fewer jobs is hardly revelatory. Historically, virtually all technical changes have had this effect (and we examine some of the suggested reasons for this in Chapter 3). If we take the view that this particular technological change is just another step along a continuous evolutionary path, then we have every reason to believe that history will repeat itself and new industries and new production processes will compensate for the decrease. If, however, the new technology has certain characteristics that make it qualitatively different, then perhaps we are witnessing the start of a discontinuous change, which may also be qualitatively different and may require us to examine the future nature of work itself. Paradoxically, it is those authors who claim the most for the new technology and hail it as a true technological 'revolution' that is to change our lives, who are more likely to place their faith in the emergence of a hitherto unknown mystery industry that will take the stresses and social strains out of this technical and historical shift. We return to these points in Chapter 9.

The second criticism we have also encountered before in the story of the British Civil Service computers; in its more familiar guise we can call it the Xerox argument. When photocopiers became widely available, numerous predictions were made of the drastic effects these would have on the demand for copy-typists. In reality, the photocopier resulted in an increase in the paperwork in circulation in the office, an increase in the number of tasks that office personnel could not perform, and no diminution in demand for typing staff (who continued to increase in numbers). Thus, it is argued that computerization will increases the number of services that the office can provide, and that the increased productivity of the new equipment will be more than offset by such additional work. This is not really a counterargument, but rather selective use of historical changes. Only time will tell us if it has wider validity.

A more substantive criticism is that the time-scale for some of the more spectacular predictions is a little vague—sometimes one gets the impression that anything with the year 2000 in the title will evoke enough science fiction imagery to cloak the prediction with respectability. More prosaically, Green and his colleagues have argued that for a community to plan an adjustment strategy towards technologically induced shifts in its occupational structure, 10 years is a more solid basis to work on.[12] On this premise, they calculated that for Tameside, Greater Manchester, England, new technology would affect the industrial mix of the locality and lead to a decline in jobs equal to 3.5%–9% of the workforce by 1990; a more modest figure than some we have encountered so far, but nevertheless disturbing.

The last major criticism of the overkill approach to unemployment is that although employment in some areas (e.g., cash registers, Swiss watches) undoubtedly has been decimated, to use a few instances as the basis for analysis of aggregate employment trends leads to a severe overestimate of the rate of diffusion. As the results of empirical studies began to be available in the early 1980s, it became clear new technology was not universally flooding into every workplace. In some sectors it was nonexistent, in others it was trickling in by dribs and drabs. As late as 1983, only 1 in 30 British companies had introduced some form of office automation.[13]

This slow rate of diffusion itself became the subject for debate as some argued that a rapid rate of diffusion would prevent a society from adjusting to change, resulting in drastic social and economic upheaval, whereas others argued that if the rate of diffusion in a given society such as the United Kingdom was too slow, it would become uncompetitive in world markets and thus lose even more jobs.

What is the person in the street to make of this plethora of prediction and counterprediction? The manager who wants to know the likely staffing implications of adopting new equipment? The employee who wants to know if his or her job is on the line?

Green and his colleagues have usefully summarized the source of some of the confusion by taking us through the mechanics of job loss.[14]

Jobs in the Ring: Down but not Out

For a job at risk to become an addition to the unemployment figures at least two things have to happen. First, the workers actually have to be laid off or made redundant. Second, there have to be no other jobs available which those workers can go to. Therefore in theory, jobs at risk can be prevented from becoming jobs lost at several stages in the process, as Figure 3 demonstrates.

However the picture is still more complicated than this diagram suggests. Overstaff and other protective practices instituted through trade union resistance may lead to lack of competitiveness if restricted to only some of the firms in the market, and thus perhaps to job loss in the long term. Also, natural wastage (or attrition) of employees who leave for a variety of personal reasons and forms of withdrawal from the labor market such as early retirement, are both means by which the current unemployment figures may be kept down, but they still result in a reduction in the *stock* of jobs available to labor market

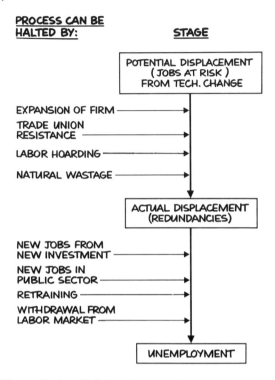

Figure 3. The mechanics of job loss. (Adapted from Green *et al.*, 1980, p. 121.)

entrants such as school-leavers or women wishing to return after a period of childrearing. Thus, in the first half of the diagram there is only one realistic way jobs can be prevented from becoming ex-jobs, and that is through the expansion of the activities of the firm. Similarly, in the second half displaced jobs can only be prevented from adding to unemployment through the rise of new jobs and retraining. As the Tameside study points out, both of these solutions run counter to what is currently the prevailing trend in many of the countries being affected by change. This brings us back to the economic context in which change takes place.

Jobless Growth

Whereas the rate of diffusion can be affected by factors such as whether the advantages of the technology are immediately perceived by economic decision-makers, and whether adequate training is available to provide the necessary labor force to operate it, the major determinant is undoubtedly the economic climate.

In a survey in the early 1980s of the take-up of microelectronics in firms in Southeast England,[15] 27% of managers, when asked what impediments there were to using new technology, replied they knew of no applications for it, and 28% gave reasons that all could be termed financial—the unavailability of funds, the general economic climate, excessive cost.

The current sluggishness of economic activity is having a major effect on diffusion, resulting in the new technology not as yet being used to create the wide range of new products that it is capable of, but rather as a replacement technology to reduce the costs of the production of existing goods and services. The main effect of this seems to be what a British Manpower Services Commission report[16] calls "jobless growth." Although not leading to immediate redundancy, the increase in productivity of the new technology is not matched by an increase in employment. The same report agrees with other studies[17] that in the short term the main depressant on levels of employment in the industrialized nations is undoubtedly the current world recession. Braun and Senker (1982) conclude that in this climate new technology looks extremely unlikely to increase employment, although this is not the same thing as saying that it would create unemployment.[18]

If, in the short run, predictions of a high level of technology-inspired redundancy seem unfounded or contradictory, why then are the unions in the industrial nations so suspicious of new technology? Is it some innate conservatism, an unformulated suspicion of all change?

The answer lies in the different perspective taken by economists and politicians on the one hand, who tend to be concerned with aggregate levels of activity in the economy as a whole, and that taken by the trade unions on the other, who are always primarily concerned with sectoral interests, that is, with their members in specific occupations in specific industries and specific locations.

There is of course no reason to assume if the overall level of employment is static or even changing at a constant rate, this will apply to the position of every sector within the economy. We have already noted how, in the past, technical change has seldom had a uniform impact; it has always been more dramatic in its effects in certain areas and for certain groups.

Werneke, in a report for the International Labor Office, concludes that the current recession not only slows the rate of diffusion in the ways already mentioned, but encourages this uneven take-up of new technology.[19] Unless the potential saving clearly outweighs the cost of investment, management may be fairly cautious or unenthusiastic about adopting innovative systems. This would seem to indicate that, although new technology has *potential* applications in all sectors of the economy, only some groups of workers will, in the initial stages, actually experience it acutely. It is of course just such disaggregated groups of the workforce that the trade unions are organized to represent.

FOCUSING DOWN

The difficulty in identifying these groups comes from the processes of official classification.

We can delineate a nation's workforce in several different ways. Standard breakdown (e.g., the British Department of Employment Standard Industrial Classification, or the U.S. Bureau of Labor) is through industry or economic activity; for example, mining, metal manufacture, or clothing and footwear. The limitation of this breakdown is that it tells us who people work for (e.g., mining companies, textile firms), but it does not tell us what they do. Thus a typist for the British National Coal Board is classified as a mining worker, such groups as cleaners would figure in all industries.

Additionally, as illustrated in the example of banking and retailing, it is the potential of new technology for cutting across the boundaries of the conventional classifications that causes us to look at the types of *jobs* that are affected. Although these tend not to be collected so frequently, a breakdown of the working population by occupation, taking Britain as a representative industrial society, comes close to that given in Table 1. The majority of the reports already cited are agreed that those areas where change occurs will be amongst those groups of workers who do what computers do best (i.e., process information) and work in areas that have to now remained labor-intensive, such as retailing and clerical work.

We will examine one of these—the special case of the office, which has undoubtedly been spotlighted as the most likely locus of rapid change.

Table 1. Structure of the Employed Population by Occupation and Gender[a]

| | Gender (percentage) | | |
Occupation	Men	Women	All
Professional and managerial	7	3	5
Professional in education, welfare, health	5	14	9
Literary, artistic, sports	1	1	1
Professional in science, engineering, and technology	7	1	4
Management	13	6	10
Clerical and related	7	30	16
Selling	4	10	7
Security & protective services	3	0	2
Catering, cleaning, hairdressing, and other personal services	4	23	12
Farming and fishing	3	1	2
Processing, making, repairing (all industries)	25	6	17
Painting, repetitive assembly, product inspecting, packaging	4	4	4
Construction and mining	6	0	4
Transport, materials moving, storing	9	1	6
Miscellaneous	2	0	2
Total	100	100	100

[a] Source: Office of Population, Censuses and Surveys, Labor Force Survey, Her Majesty's Stationery Office, London (1986).

The Office: A Suitable Case for Treatment

For most industrial societies since the second World War, the fastest growing area of employment has been that of office clerical and administrative work, the so-called "white-collar" sector. The reasons for this growth are varied, but include the expansion in the role of central and local government in Western societies, epitomized by the growth of socialized health and welfare services, the increased size and therefore administration of industrial corporations, the general expansion in the industrial economies in the 1950s and 1960s that led to a concomitant growth in white-collar services like marketing and banking, and, perhaps ironically, the automation of manual work on the shop floor that removed the conceptual aspects of many jobs from the control of the manual worker and put them into the office and into the hands of the work-study engineer and the part-programmer.

The growth in the sheer numbers of office workers had a number of side effects that included an increasing specialization of function in the office—the emergence of grades of employees who *just* did typing or just did filing, and a general lowering of the status of the clerk. These trends lay behind the rapid growth in white-collar trade unionism in the postwar era which, in the case of many of the older industrial nations such as Britain, more than made up for the decline in both employment and union membership in the older manual extractive and productive sectors.

With the lowering of the status of office work, there came also a switch in the sexual composition of the labor force as the bulk of routine office jobs came to be socially defined as "female" jobs.[20] By the end of the 1970s in the UK, 70% of all clerical workers and 98.6% of typists and secretaries were female.

Despite the growth in employment in the office sector, the technology of the office remained virtually unchanged. Until recently, the number of technological innovations in the office in the twentieth century (e.g., the typewriter, the telephone, the photocopier) could almost be counted on the fingers of one hand. A report for the ILO quoted typical clerical workers as being supported by just $2,000 worth of equipment, whereas their colleagues on the shopfloor were backed by 15 or 20 times that amount.[21] The work of the office remained, as it had been in the nineteenth century, based on paper and people. Office work is still among the most labor-intensive in the economy and thus, although productivity on the shop floor was pushed steadily upward, that of the office, although difficult to measure, remained fairly low and fairly static.

Studies in the United States estimate that from 1960–1970 the productivity of manual workers rose by 83%, whereas that of office workers rose by just 4%. The office had thus become a bottleneck in the overall efficiency of the organization and, by the 1970s, those managers who had previously seen an expanding plethora of private secretaries and other white-collar minions as a sign of status or an indication that the firm was "getting on," began to have the cost of this nonproductive labor pointed out to them by their accountants. The typical U.S. company's office costs at this time had risen to 40–50% of total costs, of which only 10% represented the cost of office equipment, 84% being labor costs.[22]

The new information technology suddenly offers the possibility of changing all this, and the hitherto undercapitalized office presents to management a significant chance to increase overall productivity for comparatively little investment outlay (compared to say the cost of retooling a car-assembly line with robots). Thus, most analysts of the new technology are unanimous in seeing the office as the area where we can expect some of the more rapid and fundamental changes. Barron and Curnow, for example, felt in 1980 that the direct price-competitiveness of office automation (compared to the price of labor) would ensure that office automation became a reality within a period of between 10 and 15 years.[23]

The hardware components of the new information technology are many and varied and should best be seen as a merging of the separate technologies of office equipment, computers, and telecommunications. As has been well documented, the technology now exists to network all the separate loci of inputting, storage, retrieval, processing, and transmitting of information in the office into one electronic information flow, the major principle of which is to ensure that:

> A task is done once only, and the information is entered at the immediate point where it arises, then automatically disseminated to all other points when and where it is required.[14]

Despite this technical potential, relatively few organizations have so far taken the plunge and gone in for a completely electronic office. More typically, they have settled for piecemeal introduction of individual items, or the computerization of specific functions—the replacement of typing by word-processing being the most popular. This means that so far only some grades of office workers have had to adjust to technological change.

It is hardly surprising that the focus for most empirical studies of office automation so far has been the word-processor. It is by far the most common item of information technology (IT) to have been introduced, and it drastically alters the work of the most typical of office workers, the typist. Its superior productivity has been pushed by the hardware suppliers who are fond of producing charts to show that the average secretary/typist only spends $x\%$ of his or her time in actually typing, compared to which the word processor can give increases in productivity of anything from 150–400%.

Predictions of the likely effects on office employment are again extremely varied. Emma Bird, in a study for the British Equal Opportunities Commission, predicted a drop of 17% in typing and secretarial jobs by 1990,[25] the even gloomier Siemens Report "Buro 2000" has already been referred to, and in Britain in the 1970s there were some well-publicized cases of organizations halving their typing staff virtually overnight through the establishment of word-processing pools.

Again, however, before extrapolating from these examples, we need to be sure that we are comparing like with like. Although as we have already noted, office jobs occur in every category in the Standard Industrial Classification, not all "offices" are the same or work in the same way.

Green et al.[26] usefully divide up office work into three areas, all with a different likelihood of being affected by IT. The first area is what can be termed the *clerical industries,* such as mail-order firms, insurance companies, banks, and public administration. This area is typified by large concentrations of office workers in single locations, and large numbers employed over all. Their main function is the production and processing of information *per se,* unlike offices in the manufacturing section where the information "shadows" the productive activity. Therefore because office activity is not tied to production, there is greater scope for organizational change, most typically represented by the separation of the purely clerical from the administrative aspects of office work, with the establishment of centralized word-processing pools.

Second, Green et al. identify the *service office,* which can be either local branches or some of the concerns in the first area (banks, insurance offices and so on) or small professional offices such as lawyers. Here the scale of operation is much smaller and thus labor displacement less likely, unless as in the case of bank branches, they can be hooked into a larger information network.

Finally, there are the manufacturing offices where the typing requirements are much smaller and most office work is multifunctional. Firms may reject word processing because they feel the volume of standard correspondence is far too small, and is already adequately handled by the photocopier.

It is the clerical industries that are clearly the most likely candidates for technological transformation; these are also the industries wherein white-collar unionization is strongest. Local government, the civil service, and increasingly banking have been much stronger growth centers for union membership than the smaller professional or manufacturing offices, the majority of which remain un-unionized. It was perhaps the frightening examples of what word-processors did to employment in the 1970's that put the clerical unions on their guard and, as we shall see in Chapter 4, promoted a flurry of new-technology bargaining. This perhaps explains why there have been few subsequent examples of massive job loss, even though the demand for typists may have slowed. In Figure 3, the experience of office automation offers some good examples of reasons why the beginnings of technological change have not as yet led to massive white-collar redundancy. There is some evidence for an expansion in work: studies of word-processor use in the United States showed that in the early stages all sorts of "hidden" work came to the fore, tasks that the office should have been doing previously but just did not have the clerical support for.[27] There are also instances of bank tellers taking on more varied and different types of tasks once computerization had reduced the time necessary for their normal telling duties. These examples should not be taken as the norm, however. More typical is the practice of accommodating job displacement either by natural wastage or by redeployment to other departments. As we saw in Figure 3, this is a short-term measure that still results in the loss of job opportunities to future potential entrants into the job market.

The position so far seems to confirm the predictions of "jobless growth"—large sections of the white-collar market are becoming a steadily shrinking or static pool of jobs rather than the source of expanding employment they once were.

Lest the absence of mass redundancy makes us too complacent and encouraged to feel that office automation has all been a big fuss over nothing, it is as well to remind ourselves that so far we are in the early stages of change. In these early stages, as was stated, new jobs are likely to be created in order for the new systems to get established. Job loss to any degree usually occurs once the systems are installed and running, and once the individual items of office automation start getting networked together. Until that time, offices still need people to act as the contact between the items of information-processing equipment.

There are also likely to be geographical consequences from widespread office automation due to the ability of new technology to transcend the confines of specific work locations. The heavy concentration of white-collar staff in government tax offices or social security centers in a few towns may be a thing of the past if the different functions of these agencies can be decentralized and relocated. Similarly, there is no longer any necessity for manufacturing concerns to maintain large prestigious offices in high-cost city-center sites. Apart from a small "front" office, the bulk of office services can be moved downtown, or out to the country, connected through computer lines.

It seems doubtful whether most of the increases in office productivity will come about simply through the introduction of new equipment. More significant is the opportunity this affords for reorganization and restructuring of office work. Information technology increasingly brings in its wake the measurement and evaluation of office working methods using the principles of work-study only previously encountered on the shop floor.

The consequences of this may come as a nasty shock to some managers. Peitchinis[29] believes that managers are too used to calculating office costs by counting in staff alone, whereas the bulk of the costs of the typical office are managerial costs. What do managers do? They spend a lot of their time assessing data and making choices on the basis of that assessment: tasks that computers can do very adequately. Peitchinis (1983) goes so far as to say that office automation will not be cost-effective unless management is subject to automation also.

This, quite frankly, seems a very distant prospect at the present time. Nevertheless, work-study and work-measurement and the reorganization of the office along the Taylorian principles (see Chapter 3, p. 65) of these branches of management science, clearly has implications for the content of work and any job satisfactions or dissatisfactions that may be derived from it.

Women—Left Holding the Baby?

Throughout the previous section, we saw that any employment effects on the office were unlikely to be spread equally over all office staff, but taking the recognized division between managerial and administrative jobs on one hand and customer-service and routine clerical jobs on the other, it was the latter group that was likely to be the focus of automation and computerization. The distinction goes deeper than this, however, when it is recognized that the former group of jobs are overwhelmingly filled by men, and the latter group by women.

This gender stratification is of course not limited to the office; especially in the postwar period, when there has been an increasing trend of women entering the labor market, the labor markets of the industrial nations have demonstrated a marked segregation by sex. Women are concentrated into an extremely limited range of occupations. Werneke (1983) quotes an Australian study that found that 85% of employed women were to be found in only 18 of 61 occupational groups listed by the Australian Statistical Office.[29]

These jobs have certain characteristics: They are likely to be in

Table 2. Percentage of Female Labor Force by Occupation[a]

Country	Clerical	Sales	Professional and technical	Administration and managerial	Service workers
Federal Republic of Germany	31.0	13.2	13.8	1.5	16.9
France	26.9	10.4	19.7	1.5	15.3
Italy	14.4	12.4	13.1	0.2	13.5
United Kingdom	30.8	12.2	12.2	0.9	23.3
United States	34.3	6.8	15.2	5.9	21.0
Canada	34.0	10.5	19.3	4.8	18.0
Australia	33.7	13.0	14.4	2.7	15.5

[a] Source: Werneke (1983), *Microelectronics and office jobs*, p. 30.

the tertiary (service) sector or in nonmanual areas (shown in Table 2); they are likely to be jobs classified as being relatively low-skilled, and will be lower paying jobs. Not only is the range of jobs narrow, but these jobs have often become "feminized," that is, over 50% of people doing that job are women. In many cases, such as typing and secretarial work, these jobs are almost solely done by women.

These 'feminized' jobs are in many cases exactly those areas that are estimated the most likely to be computerized. How this works is evident if we return to the office. Werneke usefully suggests that we can divide all "information sector" jobs into those which create and analyze information (the "skilled end" of the information spectrum and predominantly male) and those who manipulate information (secretaries, typists, cashiers), in other words, those areas of concentrated female employment. Microelectronics is fundamentally conceived of as an aid to those in the creative end to assist their decision-making by speeding up and widening the information flow. For the information handlers, they are being required to step up their productivity in the supply of information, one route of which may be to minimize the number of handlers as much as possible.

Therefore, to return to the process of analysis of employment effects which we started by looking at aggregate effects, followed by examination of those industries most likely to be affected, and then the jobs within those industries, if we now ask, "who *does* these jobs at present?" we get a picture similar to Figure 4.

This of course is not meant to give the impression that only women will be threatened with the loss of their jobs, or that all women employed in these sectors are at risk. In fact, the characteristics of the

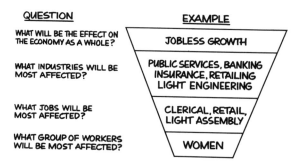

QUESTION

WHAT WILL BE THE EFFECT ON
THE ECONOMY AS A WHOLE?

WHAT INDUSTRIES WILL BE
MOST AFFECTED?

WHAT JOBS WILL BE
MOST AFFECTED?

WHAT GROUP OF WORKERS
WILL BE MOST AFFECTED?

EXAMPLE

JOBLESS GROWTH

PUBLIC SERVICES, BANKING
INSURANCE, RETAILING
LIGHT ENGINEERING

CLERICAL, RETAIL,
LIGHT ASSEMBLY

WOMEN

Figure 4. Focusing the employment effects.

female labor market are such that actual redundancies could appear very small in number. Because society still ascribes to working women with children two roles, worker and mother, which traditionally have been held to be incompatible (whereas the roles of worker and father have not), it is still normal for women to drop out of the labor market for periods of socially prescribed child-care, and then seek to return into the market at a later date. This high turnover of female labor means that it is relatively easy for managers to reduce the stock of jobs on IT-affected departments through natural wastage and the nonfilling of vacancies. This also means that large areas of employment that traditionally offered avenues back into the labor market to married women could become closed to them.

These characteristics of the female section of the labor market mean that adjustment to these employment effects may not be easy for women. First, there is still a very narrow range of occupations that are widely open to women and many of these are likely to be IT-affected. Second, the demands of childrearing and the external timetables of school or nursery hours, feeding, and bedtimes mean that women may not feel free to accept jobs outside normal working hours or jobs that are over a certain number of miles away.

The new job areas that will be created as a result of the growth of computerization unfortunately at present do not hold out much hope for women. Growth areas like programming, systems analysis, data management, or electronic engineering are overwhelmingly male in composition. A Swedish study, for example, found that 90% of data-processing managers were men, as were 80% of data processing planners, whereas 97% of routine data entry posts were female (and they of course are likely candidates for automation themselves).[30]

It has been suggested that this must be because there are few women with the necessary technological skills and that the answer lies in more training and encouragement for women to enter areas such as computing and engineering. The reasons may lie deeper than this— Cooley (1987) has suggested that the very emphasis which our societies place on technology for its own sake and the uses to which we put it (military and exploitative) reflect dominant values that may be termed male: man as hunter, tamer of nature, and so on.[31]

Also it must be said that as long as hardware manufacturers continue to use women to sell their equipment by portraying them draped over the magic boxes in a variety of nonproductive postures, or depict them continually in a servicing role, then any fully qualified female computer-systems analyst is going to have an uphill struggle against the boys in the DP department.

SUNRISE, SUNSET

We noted in our examination of predictions of the aggregate employment effects of new technology that those writers who can be placed in the "optimistic" category see a technology-induced decline ("sunset") in sectors that are currently labor-intensive as just another turn in the industrial spiral, which would be more than compensated for by expansion in the microelectronic and computer "sunrise" industries themselves. Thus the American Arthur D. Little Agency concluded at the end of the 1970s that microelectronics would create an extra one million new jobs in the major industrial nations over the next decade.[32] Some regional and national economies have pinned their economic hopes firmly on such promises. The Scottish Development Agency, faced with massive decline in the old heavy infrastructural industries of coal, steel, and shipbuilding, has offered a plethora of grants and inducements to microelectronics firms to set up branches in Scotland, creating the so-called "Silicon Glen" in Scotland's central belt.

Before placing our trust in microelectronics to lead us into a new dawn of full employment, there are certain factors (such as the location, quality, and amount of new jobs) that must be taken into consideration. To understand these factors we must be a little clearer about the nature of the industries concerned.

Because there is some confusion in the general literature over what

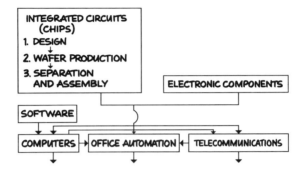

Figure 5. The information technology industries.

precisely the "sunrise industries" are or might be, I have endeavored to illustrate in Figure 5 the stages in and relationships between the major employment sectors of information technology. Within this schematic figure, there are some additional complications such as important marketing differences between those firms who produce standard high-volume general application chips and those who produce specialist custom-designed chips, or between the mainframe and micro-computer sections of the computer industry. For our purposes, however, neither the stages of production nor the types of labor employed are substantively different and will be ignored for the time being.

There are four major characteristics of the microelectronics industry or industries in general, each of which poses substantial problems for the generation of new employment: (a) The industries have a pronounced international division of labor and (b) a sexual division of labor that perpetuates the labor-market divisions noted in the previous pages; (c) they are dominated by large multinational corporations; and (d) the processes of production are subject to their own technology.

The international division of labor is of course by now a well-known feature of today's global economy and inherent in the very nature of the transnational corporation. It is therefore hardly surprising that it should be more prevalent in a newly emergent industry such as microelectronics, rather than some of the more traditional industries. This situation in itself raises a question mark over some of the equilibrium employment theories—the idea that an emergent technology, after a transitional period of adjustment to the labor market, will provide enough new job opportunities to return the system to a full-employment equilibrium. This model is very much based on an assumption of a closed economic system, a single nation state economy with few significant labor market inputs or outputs. This assumption may have been credible in the classical economic heyday of the eighteenth century (although the slave trade shows that it was not particularly valid then), but it certainly cannot be assumed today that any new jobs which are created in new or transformed industries will necessarily be in the same geographical location as the declining old ones, or even in another part of the same country to which labor can move over time.

To take a much quoted example, the European watch and clock industry was ravaged by the unforeseen arrival of the digital watch. Digital watches have proved best sellers, so cheap they are virtually given away at petrol stations when you fill up your tank. Many people who may not have possessed a watch may now have two or three. But the new watches are in general not made by the same skilled fingers that once produced pieces of mini-precision engineering, rather they are assembled in the thousands by very young girls in Hong Kong or Singapore.

The international division of labor is best exemplified in the manufacture of the integrated circuits (ICs) or microchips themselves, the major stages of which are shown in Figure 5. The majority of the world's microchips are still designed in America, many in the now famous Silicon Valley in California, although the efforts of European and Japanese governments to develop their "national" chips have slightly dented the American control of circuit design. (If, however, we count in the world's largest designer and producer of chips, IBM, America still dominates the market; IBM, of course, does not sell any of its chips but uses them all in its own products.) In a process now frequently described, ICs are then etched many, many times over into round wafers of silicon in production plants that are mostly located in the Western industrial economies. The labor-intensive part of the job however, where the hundreds of chips are separated from each wafer and then assembled onto mountings, is almost invariably performed in the low wage-cost countries of Southeast Asia.

The history of electronics corporations' involvement in Southeast Asia goes back two decades to the era of the transistor, when Fairchild opened a facility in Hong Kong in 1963 and was followed by other companies into Taiwan, Singapore, and South Korea. In the 1970s, the second wave of development expanded to Malaysia, Thailand, the Phillipines, and Indonesia. In these offshore assembly plants, it is not uncommon for the women to work an 84-hour week in 12-hour shifts.

Wages in Hong Kong electronics factories at the start of the 1980s were about $45 per day, in the Phillipines about 86 cents.

Just as the labor-intensive stage of the production becomes located in areas where the historically won conventions of industrial employment do not apply, so the "creative" or skilled side of the business becomes located in what are already high-wage, high-employment areas. In the United Kingdom, for example, 45% of all software programmers and systems analysts are located in the relatively prosperous Southeast of England, rather than in traditional industrial areas of the North, Wales, and Scotland, which have suffered most job loss.

This geographical division of labor is paralleled by the familiar gender distinctions between the creative and the routine assembly side of the industries. The Southeast Asian workers of Motorola, National Semiconductor, and Texas Instruments, described above are almost totally female, their loyalty to the company emphasized by company beauty shows and the stressing of "female" qualities such as docility and passivity. Similarly, in the Silicon Valley itself, in one of the richest states in the richest country in the world, whereas the research and design staff were nearly all highly paid men, a trade-union survey showed that the typical assembly worker was female, did not have English as her first language, is between 18 and 30 years old, was likely to be on welfare because her wages were only just above the legal minimum.[33]

The microelectronics companies have the resources to choose the most favorable locations for their processes, because they are big. Much of the mythology of the "sunrise" industry is still retelling the success stories of the 1960s when the early semiconductor companies were starting. The idea that the industry today offers chances of success to small innovative companies run by a couple of young whiz-kids is simply not true. United States estimates of the chances of a new product entering the market are 1 in 20, and once a small company does come up with something, the large companies are quick to buy it up. At the start of the 1980s, just five companies, excluding IBM, produced 80% of the U.S. chip production—Texas Instruments, Fairchild, Motorola, Intel, and National Semiconductor. In the mainframe computer industry, the concentration is even more marked, with IBM holding about 64% of the world market.[34]

The sheer pace of technological development and the increasing sophistication of the hardware means that the resources necessary for research and development become formidable obstacles not only for those wishing to set up new companies, but even for established companies wishing to swim with the technological tide. The rate of mortality of small and medium-sized new technology companies remains very high, as evidenced by the ups and downs of much acclaimed "home micro" companies, whereas in the large computer end of the industry, large companies like General Electric and RCA pulled out altogether.

The size of the companies and the rapid turnaround of products makes the location of production an almost constantly changing process. Companies like Honeywell, Burroughs, NCR, and ITT have been interested in the past in moving to regions like Scotland because of the grants and inducements available, but as their products have changed, the new products have often been established in new plants somewhere else with a drastic pruning of the workforce as a result.

This process has been accelerated by the fact that the industry is subject to its own technology: Computers now design and help to build computers, robots build robots. With the shift from electromechanical to fully electronic components, most of the big companies actually reduced their workforces in the late 1970s, at the very time when the microelectronic revolution was getting underway. Thus, in the U.K. computer industry there were 10,000 less people employed in 1977 than there had been in 1971 and the U.K. electronic-components industry dropped from 153,000 to 129,000 in the 3 years leading to 1977.[35] Over the 10 years leading to 1978, employment in top office-automation companies fell by 40% (NCR), 35% (Olympia Werke), 20% (Alder Werke), 18% (Smith-Corona Machines), and 10% (Olivetti).[36]

The search for bigger and better chips has within it, if not the seeds of its own destruction, then certainly an inner paradox. As Peter Large put it, "If one chip tomorrow will do the work of twenty today, then who will buy the other nineteen?"[37] He counters this, however, by pointing out that in the early years of computers some very eminent mathematicians worked out that the world would only ever need about a dozen computers at the most.

DISCUSSION QUESTIONS

1. Why is the statement "technology causes unemployment" misleading?
2. What specific features of information technology could affect both the level and structure of employment?
3. Why is it that the jobs of women workers are more likely to be adversely affected by the introduction of information technology into the workplace?

4. What conditions would need to be fulfilled in order that IT-based industries could replace the older "smokestack" industries as sources of employment?

REFERENCES

1. Central Policy Review Staff, *Social and employment implications of microelectronics,* Her Majesty's Stationery Office, London (1978), p. 3.
2. N.D. Kondratiev, The long waves in economic life, *Lloyds Bank Review, 129,* July 1978, pp. 41–60.
3. B. Wilkinson, *The shopfloor politics of new technology,* Heinemann, London (1983), pp. 9–16.
4. Central Policy Review Staff, *Social and employment implications of microelectronics,* Her Majesty's Stationery Office, London (1978).
5. T. Stonier, *The third industrial revolution,* International Metalworkers Federation, Vienna (1979).
6. I. Barron & R. Curnow, *The future with microelectronics,* Open University Press, Milton Keynes (1979), pp. 189–192.
7. J. Rada, *The impact of microelectronics,* International Labor Office, Geneva (1980), p. 26.
8. S. Nora & A. Minc, *The computerisation of society—A report to the President of France,* MIT Press, London (1980), pp. 35–36.
9. J. Rada, *The impact of microelectronics,* International Labor Office, Geneva (1980), p. 33.
10. S. Peitchinis, *Computer technology and employment: Retrospect & prospect,* Macmillan, London, (1983), p. 137.
11. C. Jenkins & B. Sherman, *The collapse of work,* Eyre Methuen, London (1979), p. 113.
12. K. Green, R. Coombs, & K. Holroyd, *The effects of microelectronic technologies on employment prospects: A case study of Tameside,* Gower Press, Farnborough (1980), p. 115.
13. D. Werneke, *Microelectronics & office jobs—The impact of the chip on women's employment,* International Labor Office, Geneva (1983), p. 22.
14. K. Green, R. Coombs & K. Holroyd, *The effects of microelectronic technologies on employment prospects,* Gower Press, Farnborough (1980).
15. T. Bourner, H. Davies, V. Lintner, A. Woods, & M. Woods, *The diffusion of microelectronic technology in south-east England,* in: D. Bosworth (ed.), *The employment consequences of technical change,* Macmillan, London (1983).
16. E. Braun & P. Senker, *New technology and employment,* Manpower Services Commission, London (July, 1982), pp. 2.2–3.2.
17. Council for Science & Society, *New technology: Society, employment and skill—Report of a working party,* Author, London (1981).
18. E. Braun & P. Senker, *New technology and employment,* Manpower Services Commission, London (July, 1982).
19. D. Werneke, *Microelectronics and office jobs,* International Labor Office, Geneva (1983), pp. 21–24.
20. D. Werneke, *Microelectronics and office jobs,* International Labor Office, Geneva (1983), p. 28.

21. J. Rada, *The impact of microelectronics,* International Labor Office, Geneva (1980), p. 31.
22. E. Braun & P. Senker, *New technology and employment,* Manpower Services Commission, London (July, 1982), p. 5.15.
23. I. Barron & R. Curnow, *The future with microelectronics,* Open University Press, Milton Keynes (1979), pp. 142–154.
24. Association of Professional, Executive, Clerical & Computer Staff, *Automation and the office worker,* Author, London (1980), p. 10.
25. E. Bird, *Information technology in the office: The impact on womens' jobs,* Equal Opportunities Commission, Manchester (1980).
26. K. Green, R. Coombs & K. Holroyd, *The effects of microelectronic technologies on employment prospects,* Gower, Farnborough (1980), pp. 25–27.
27. EDP Analyzer, The experience of word processing, in: T. Forester (ed.), *The microelectronics revolution* Basil Blackwell, Oxford (1980), pp. 232–243.
28. S. G. Peitchinis, *Computer technology and employment,* Macmillan, London (1983), pp. 51–53.
29. D. Werneke, *Microelectronics and office jobs,* International Labor Office, Geneva (1983), p. 31.
30. D. Werneke, *Microelectronics and office jobs,* International Labor Office, Geneva (1983), p. 34.
31. M. Cooley, *Architect or bee?,* Hogarth Press, London (1987), pp. 87–89.
32. Association of Professional Executive Clerical & Computer Staff, *Automation and the office worker,* Author, London (1980), p. 28.
33. M. Duncan, Microelectronics: Five areas of subordination, L. Levidow & B. Young (eds.) *Science, Technology and the Labour Process,* CSE Books, London (1981), pp. 172–207.
34. J. Rada, *The impact of microelectronics,* International Labor Office, Geneva (1980), pp. 37–39.
35. National Computing Centre & AUEW/TASS, *Computer technology and employment,* Author, Manchester (1979), p. 117.
36. J. Rada, *The impact of microelectronics,* International Labor Office, Geneva (1980), p. 38.
37. P. Large, *The micro revolution revisited,* Frances Pinter, London (1984).

3

THE QUALITY OF WORK AND THE WORKING ENVIRONMENT

People are trouble, but machines obey.
The Engineer, September 14, 1978

If the predictions as to the effects on employment were diverse, those relating to the effects on the quality of working life are perhaps even more so, ranging from a vision of future new-technology-based work being intrinsically much more satisfying, creative, and skilled than the majority of jobs created by industrialism, to the countervision of the future worker as a bored, alienated, deskilled appendage to a terminal, routinely performing only a small part of some monstrous information process.

The difficulty of producing a less emotional assessment than these starts with the fact that notions of what is a "satisfying" job are inevitably essentially subjective: what may be satisfying to me may be the opposite to you. To overcome this problem, much of the vast socio-psychological literature on "job satisfaction" does one of two things.

It either starts with a model of what the individual human being ideally desires (for example the theories of Maslow or Herzberg), and then assesses a given job against this model, or it takes the attitudes toward their work expressed by workers and then suggests ways of modifying the jobs to modify the attitudes. Most of these attempts are guilty of two failings. First, they do not analyze the nature of jobs themselves and the assumptions and priorities that may be built into the way they are designed (see Chapter 5), but instead simply measure the degree to which workers have adjusted to the jobs. Second, given the essentially psychological basis of many of these studies, they are concerned mainly with the interface between the individual worker and an individual job and thus are in danger of neglecting the social relationships in which work is embedded.

Therefore, in attempting to analyze the relationship between computer-based technological change and the quality of working life, we must begin in a way that hopefully avoids some of these pitfalls. Put simply, we can say that the quality of work as experienced by the worker is a product of two interrelated factors: the content and the context.

The content of a job is made up of several overlapping factors, including its composition of differing amounts of mental and manual activity, the degree of autonomy and exercise of judgment required (and the converse, the degree to which it is closely supervised or machine-controlled), the skills required for its performance, whether it is a whole task or a single portion of a larger task, and whether it is varied or repetitive.

Similarly, the context of the job includes the working environment—whether it is pleasant or unpleasant, safe or hazardous; the social organization of work—whether the worker is isolated or is part of a social group with whom communication is possible; the authority relationship—the type and degree of supervision (clearly related to the above); and the role of the job in the organization—does it offer promotion or training prospects, or is it seen as a dead end?

Although separated here for the purposes of analysis, content and context are clearly two sides of the same coin, and supervision provides the clearest link between the two. Therefore any prediction that the quality of working life will improve or deteriorate with the adoption of information technology, must refer not only to changes in the content of work, but also in the working environment. In trying to assess, as we did with employment, whether there is any evidence so far to support either assertion, we find that much of the debate hinges around

two key concepts into which much of the above has been subsumed—
the notions of skill and control.

TOWARD A HIGH-SKILL WORKFORCE?

In attempting to learn from our historical experience of technological change we find that most writers are of the opinion that there
definitely is a relationship between such change and the overall skill
structure of the workforce, but, as with employment trends, there is
no clear agreement as to the precise nature of the relationship that will
enable us to project into the future when we combine it with our knowledge of the characteristics of microelectronics.

Braun and Senker for the Manpower Services Commission have
pointed out that there are in fact three main possibilities: (a) that the
general level of skills will rise with technological improvement, (b) that
the general level of skills will fall, or (c) that there will be a polarity
in the distribution of jobs between a highly skilled elite and a mass of
unskilled labor.[1]

It might seem at first glance that there is an obvious case for computerization and information technology leading to a general raising of
levels of skill and job satisfaction. Until recently, computers required
a high level of academic or technical training to operate: thus the spread
of computerization into more locations through their relative cheapness
and reduced size must arguably require a greater number of highly
trained operators. In addition, it is clear that computers and robotics
can do away with the necessity for people to work in hazardous or
unhealthy working conditions, and it is argued that the new jobs in the
"sunrise" industries of microelectronics are surely going to be more
pleasant and less injurious to health than the old declining heavy industries.

Protagonists of information technology who follow this line of argument stress the necessity for all of us to learn new skills to cope with
the new equipment (a theme that runs through the official stress on the
importance of training in "keyboard skills," computer literacy, etc.),
and give the impression that nearly all types of employment in the
future information society will be at a higher level of skill and intrinsic
interest than many of today's jobs. For example, the British Central
Policy Review Staff Report on microelectronics confidently predicts
that the spread of automated assembly will give the production worker

"the opportunity to aquire new skills and the freedom associated with white-collar work," whereas in the automated office "there will also be scope for re-organizing clerical operations in order to provide greater job satisfaction."[2]

This is not a new argument. Periodically, as a reaction to the clearly unsatisfactory nature of many industrial jobs, writers and observers have looked for signs of development into a new technological stage characterized by more fulfilling employment. The most widely quoted of these is the work of Robert Blauner who, in 1964, while spotlighting assembly-line work such as automobile assembly as possibly the most alienating (in his terms) form of work organization ever produced by industrial society, nevertheless saw in the new process industries (such as refining and chemicals) a development offering an increase in intrinsic satisfaction.[3] There was an assumption here and in similar approaches, that the skill required to conceive and design the technology or the product are somehow transmitted through the technology into a high level of expertise being required to *operate* it. Blauner's prediction however was subsequently demonstrated to be wrong. Many jobs remaining in a capital-intensive industry like chemicals are either highly stressful due to the social isolation involved, or consist of sheer physical, ("unskilled") labor.[4]

The idea that the level of skills in the population will continue to rise is usually based on an analysis of past occupational trends such as the increase in the proportion of white-collar work and in professional categories in the service sector. Gershuny, for example, notes in an examination of UK occupational shifts from 1961 to 1971 that the loss of semi-skilled and skilled jobs in the manufacturing and clerical sectors was more than made up for by an increase in the professional category in the service sector.[5]

These categories need to be considered very carefully before we take them at their face value; they are after all only convenient statistical groupings and they do not necessarily reflect the social reality. Braverman has pointed out that the original use of the term *semi-skilled* by Dr. A. Edwards in the United States' occupational statistics in the 1930s was to cover the large and growing body of jobs that were in some way connected with machinery; thus machine-minders and machine-watchers all became classed as *semi-skilled*. Braverman critically compares this to the declining sector of agricultural workers who were all lumped together as "laborers" despite the very real and complex skills required in agricultural work, and somewhat scathingly comments:

It is only in the world of census statistics, and not in terms of direct assessment, that an assembly-line worker is presumed to have greater skill than a fisherman or oysterman, the forklift operator greater skill than the gardener or groundskeeper . . .[6]

Similar criticisms can be made of the universal assumption that clerical work is more highly skilled than manual work. This is based on a confusion between *socially constructed* skill, or the status position that the job may have in the wider social and occupational hierarchy, and *genuine* skill, the actual level of skill and responsibility that the job may contain. Thus to award low-grade routine clerical work the same skill status as skilled engineering machine-tool operation makes little objective sense, and yet this is precisely how many national census statistics treat them.

When we actually look at such clerical jobs and analyze them in terms of the degree of repetitive action, routine movement, performance of a single fragmented task, (computer key-punch operators are a good example here), we may find that the actual task is not so very dissimilar from tasks which, if they are performed "downstairs" by fellow workers in overalls instead of office clothing, count as far less skilled.

The increasing role of the tertiary or service sector in the occupational structure (explained further in Chapter 6) gave a further boost to assumptions of increasing skill, with much emphasis being placed on the skills of personal face-to-face contacts in service jobs. Kumar has suggested that much of this may simply be a process of relabeling for reasons of increased status and prestige.[7] He gives the example of the expanding number of "professions;" while at one time these were limited to education and the law, today everyone from taxidermists to personnel managers wants to be regarded as members of a bona fide profession, each with its own professional institute. Yet how much of this constitutes evidence for a genuine increase in skill? It still remains true that if you sell cars for a living this is not seen as a profession, yet if you sell houses it is.

Although it is invalid to make sweeping generalizations from these examples, they do point our attention to the dangers of taking statistical categories too literally and perhaps may make us look a little more critically at the rosier predictions of a unilinear trend of increasing skill levels, (made often with similar generalizations on the basis of these very same categories), which microelectronics because of its high-tech nature is assumed will accelerate. For more concrete evidence, we look to the experience of workers in key areas of the new "sunrise" industries.

Peering into the Sunrise

As stated in Chapter 2, jobs in the microelectronics industries can be divided into a relatively small number of creative jobs in system design that are well paid, and the majority of jobs in the actual fabrication, assembly, and testing of the hardware. Many of these assembly jobs are located in Third World countries, especially in Southeast Asia, which suggests that the techniques required for assembly do not demand a long training period or an overall high level of educational standard in the society and that all that is important is the low cost of labor for these assembly functions; that is, that they are unskilled.

The evidence from Southeast Asia for a higher quality of working life does not look very promising. In the previous chapter we saw that the employees (predominantly female and usually teenagers) work long shifts for what in Western terms are extremely low wage rates. A tester of chips for a large multinational in Malaysia describes her job, (for which in 1979 she was paid $1 a day):

> After the training period they set my quota at 15 trays a day. Now I have to test 25 trays a day. I think there are between 160–180 chips in each tray, so I test around 3,500 chips a day . . . After six months I became sick with red-eye [conjectivitis]. I don't know why this happened. Other friends at work got sick too. The supervisor told me to clean my microscope so nobody else would get it. Then he gave me two week medical leave. While I was at home, my family all got red-eye too.[8]

In Hong Kong, most female workers in the industry are nicknamed "Grandma" because the constant use of microscopes means they usually need glasses by their early twenties.

It might be argued that we cannot take these examples as a basis for dismissing the idea that new technology will bring about improvements in the quality of work as such conditions will only prevail in Third World countries where there is not the experience of industrialism and thus "expectations" are not so high. However, we have seen that low-cost assembly is one of the foundation stones upon which the international microelectronics industry rests; we are left with the uneasy suspicion that if microelectronics jobs in the advanced industrial nations are to be predominantly high-skill, responsible, high-discretion jobs, then this will depend upon the "export" of low-skill, routine, low-paid jobs to the low-wage sectors of the global economy.

Clearly here we have entered the world of social and political values; we can either find such practices ethically unacceptable, or we can take the view that compared to the preindustrial conditions in these countries, such employment opportunities constitute an advance in the workers' standard of living.

Dubious as this latter argument is, it cannot be used of the conditions experienced in the companies at the forefront of technical development in the heart of the industry, Silicon Valley, and whose use of cheap female labor we noted in Chapter 2.[9]

There is little evidence here that the demand for low-skilled routine industrial workers has been dispensed with even in the leading edge of the industry. In addition, the first impression of working conditions in the industry, with its "clean rooms" and white working overalls, belies the fact that many of the substances, solvents and acids, used to etch the silicon are extremely toxic or hazardous. In 1987, a leading microchip manufacturer removed all female employees who were pregnant from working with these substances, owing to an above average level of birth abnormalities.

Deskilling

The second hypothesis concerning the relationship between technical change and skill levels is the direct opposite of the above, namely that automation and the continuing division of labor has steadily reduced the level of skills in the majority of jobs, transforming the workforce into a legion of machine-minders. From the very earliest criticism of industrialism, there has been considerable popular support for this point of view: that industrial jobs were increasingly of the put-bolt-a-into-hole-b variety; meaningless, alienating, monotonous, and requiring from the operative nothing except endurance. This, however, is too simple a view of skill. It sees skill as a tangible thing that is either present in a job or ceases to exist and thus if 'removed' from the job it goes somehow into nothingness.

It is therefore necessary at this point to examine what we mean by skill. The report of the Council for Science and Society working party points out that it usually implies some degree of mental control and discretion: A conditioned response (such as saluting an officer) is thus not skillful.[10] Skill largely reflects the ability to respond to the unexpected and the unpredictable and this can require a combination of physical and mental activity; thus a football player and a brain surgeon are both skillful—responding to ever-changing situations, whereas a chocolate-bar packer is merely dexterous.

Skill, therefore, inherently includes the ability to control the work process in some way; if you cannot control it, you cannot make decisions over how to tackle the job, which sequence of operations would be most effective, what pace the job should be done and so on. Now if, wherever we have used the word "skill" we used the word "control" we can see that you cannot just take control out of a job and throw it away: the job must be controlled somewhere. The operator will say that he or she is now controlled by the machine but the machine is not a force in itself—it can only do what it has been constructed or programmed to do. So what has really happened here is that control over the job—the skill formerly vested in that set of tasks—has passed from the hands of the machine operator into the hands of the designer or programmer.

If this process accurately describes what happens through the increasing use of automated and programmable technology, then it suggests that the third prediction, that of skill polarity, may be closer to reality than the other two. Here, a general lowering in the skill content of the majority of jobs could well be accompanied by an increase in either the skills required or the numbers employed in the relatively smaller programming or system design end of the productive process, reflecting a transfer of the locus of control.

In order to assess whether this hypothesis is supported by experience we will take two examples that have received a lot of attention and study; CNC machining in the area of shopfloor production, and word processing in the office.

Case Study: Computer Numerically Controlled (CNC) Machining

As we remarked in Chapter 2, the engineering machinist has been the repository of accumulated shopfloor skills built up by a combination of formal training and a lot of experience, reflected in his or her ability to interpret the engineering drawing and calculate the tooling, machining sequences, and speeds necessary for the job. Over the years, some of this calculation has been shifted into the province of the production engineer, but the manual operation of the milling machine, vertical borer, or lathe to achieve work to high levels of tolerance is still a very skilled process.

Numerically controlled (NC), and now computer numerically controlled (CNC) machine tools have altered this process fundamentally. A paper program tape, produced by technicians called "part programmers" replaces the written instructions to the machinist and drives the machine through the required sequence of motions. CNC differs from the earlier NC machines in that the control terminal contains the facility to modify or "edit" the tapes actually on the machine. Manufacturers claim that the advantages include uniformity of quality and precision, and, because several operations such as milling or boring can be performed at a single multitooled "machining center," a reduction in setup and transfer times.[11]

Clearly much of the mental process of interpreting the drawing and instructions and the experience-based skills of setting up the machine are now removed from being mainly the responsibility of the machinist to being mainly the responsibility of the programmer. So what remains of the job of the engineering machinist?

The evidence here seems confusing at first. On the one hand, an article in *American Machinist* described how a mentally handicapped young man with the IQ of a 12-year-old had become a company's star NC machine center operator because "his limitations afford him the level of patience and persistence to carefully watch his machine and the work that it produces" and because it was "the kind of tedious work that some non-handicapped people might have difficulty coping with."[12] In contrast, other studies have found the skills of machinists on CNC machines to be still required in order to reliably produce the product to the required standards.[13,14]

So what can be the explanation for the difference in reported experience? An initial determining factor would seem to be the context in which the work is performed, and particularly the product-market of the firm. Where the machine tool shop specializes in frequently changing products made in small batches these necessitate a more frequent resetting of machines, and it is fairly usual for new programs to contain bugs which only become apparent during the initial run on the machine.

Also, high quality and tolerances demanded in a product are likely to require the frequent adjustment and editing of the programs to allow for tool wear and differences in quality of raw materials, and the ex perience that enables the machinist to detect a subtle alteration in the noise pitch which may be an indicator of tool wear is essential here.

However, a requirement simply to be alert or to constantly watch the machine and hit the button if things go wrong, on its own cannot really be described as retained skill. On short runs, this could be tolerable, but clearly on a long run it could become very tedious. Now the requirement to take remedial action if the machine does go wrong has usually led the CNC machinists to feel they have to learn the essential elements of programming, and the facility that CNC offers to do this editing directly on the machine has introduced the possibility of new skills into the machinist's job.

However, there are often practical limits to the degree to which they have been able to extend their skills into this new area (where control over the job now lies). Very often such encroachment is resisted by the programmers who feel strongly that any editing of tapes is "their" job. In other firms, it is management who have decided that the machinists are not to edit tapes and have blanked over or locked up the CNC controls.[15]

We later examine the various ways in which this problem has been resolved, sometimes in favor of the machinists, sometimes in favor of the programmers. At this point in our argument however, the example strongly suggests that another determinant of whether particular elements of skill are included in a job may have more to do with organizational factors than any technological necessity that it be so.

It is worth noting here that these organizational factors can also condition the technical performance of the equipment. There are several recorded instances of downtime actually being increased with the switch to CNC due to the shopfloor working continuous shifts while the programmers, enjoying the usual "staff" conditions, only worked during the day. If a tape proves faulty or requires modification during a late shift there is often little option but to bring the machine down.

Case Study: Skill and Control in the Office

It has been alleged that it has been the continuous process of the removal of control from shopfloor operations that has been partly responsible for the steady expansion of office employment. The need for the processing of time-cards, job-sheets, work-flow schedules, and the coordination of a thousand fragmented sub-tasks has made the office the "paper replica of the production process."[16] Now this replica is being rendered invisible through the use of electronic technology.

As we noted in Chapter 2, the office has remained relatively immune from technological change and so many of those issues which emanate from change and which have traditionally been so much a part of shopfloor industrial relations (demarcation, regrading, staffing levels, work speeds) have until recently been relatively absent from industrial relations in the office. Now that office work is being transformed through computerization and office automation, clerical workers are for the first time being forced to examine these and other issues and, in so doing, to reexamine the very nature and content of clerical work itself.

Office work has several distinctive characteristics in both its organization and its social relations. This becomes clear if we first compare it with the organizational classifications most commonly used to describe shopfloor production:

1. Small batch, as for example in much of the engineering industry, where the product is made to a customer's specifications and thus is characterized by frequent changes and modifications.

2. Large batch where, although the product changes, this is only following relatively long runs of production—good examples are automobiles or textiles.

3. Process production, such as is found in chemicals or public utilities like gas and electricity supply, where the production process is a continuous flow through capital-intensive and product-specific plants in which retooling for a different product would be expensive or impossible.

Although there are difficulties with these categories, the major drawback is that they exclusively refer to the production areas in the organization, reflecting the hitherto low level of academic or managerial interest in the analysis of clerical work. It has been suggested that office work comes closest to representing process production, the "product" here being information, which is constantly processed in an endless flow. The major difference between an office process and an industrial process is of course that the former is primarily labor-intensive.

The social relations in the office are characterized mostly by the pronounced gender difference between the managerial, decision-making, high-discretion jobs that are predominantly filled by males, and the routine clerical and secretarial, low-discretion jobs which are predominantly filled (98% in the UK[17]) by females. This distinction is so pronounced and so apparently universal in Western industrial societies that it has been suggested that the normal authority relationship between worker and supervisor has in the office been either reinforced by or replaced by patriarchal relationships that gain their authority from the dominant male status in the wider society. Thus the secretary is not just the manager's subordinate but becomes the "office wife," making him coffee, watering the office plants, protecting him from hostile callers, making sure he keeps the right engagements. In Japan, where patriarchal attitudes in the wider society are even stronger than in Europe and North America, female secretarial staff are actually referred to as "shokuba no hana" or "office flowers" and are chosen for their submissiveness and decorative qualities.

The perplexing thing about such arrangements is that they are not very cost effective. While having his own personal secretary has been the traditional way in which the manager has marked his status in the organizational hierarchy (and in turn it has been his status rather than her abilities at typing and shorthand that has provided her own source of internal status), the employment of highly competent secretarial staff for the sort of practices outlined above hardly represents the most efficient utilization of labor, especially when compared to the rigid policing of every unproductive minute spent by shopfloor production workers. This of course pales into insignificance when compared to the waste of talent represented by the unwillingness or inability of companies to recruit or promote women to managerial positions.

When this characteristic is combined with the labor-intensity of office work it becomes clear why the office has been discovered to be a bottleneck in company profitability and thus a likely target for automation. So, when computers and other items of office automation are introduced into this context, what evidence is there so far as to the most likely effects on office workers' job content and satisfaction?

Concentrating on the most widely discussed item of office automation, the word processor, a major consequence of the switch to word processing seems undoubtedly to be an increase in specialization and the functional division of labor. The typical office secretary's work can be divided into correspondence work (mainly typing) and administrative work (such as filing and managing small accounts), while other duties such as using and answering the telephone may fall into both categories. Administrative duties are usually seen as being more skilled, and a common career pattern for the office secretary has been to start as a typist and gradually acquire more office skills with the hope of eventually becoming a personal secretary (in most cases the end of the promotional ladder for female office staff).

This frequently seems to change with the switch to word processing. One U.S. multinational broke down their headquarters' secretarial jobs into several specialized discrete parts following the introduction of word processing: one woman typed all day, another only did electronic filing, another answered phones and so on, the staff rotating to another subtask after a few months.[18]

More usually, despite the increased awareness of health and safety requirements, word processor operators frequently do nothing else but type.[19] A frequently quoted advertisement by a leading hardware manufacturer actually refers to all the nontyping duties performed by the traditional secretary (and claimed to amount to as much as 98% of the time) to emphasize the increased productivity which word processing can bring.[20] The word-processor operator no longer needs to move around to file away documents or consult past files as this can all be done electronically on the screen and disc drive. If the printer is located in another office, he or she may never even get to see or to handle the finished document.

This specialization and the removal of even elementary "administrative" functions adjacent to the typing function means that often the operator now no longer gets to see and understand the whole job done in the office, but only a detached part of it, just like colleagues on the factory floor. It also effectively cuts the operator off from the gradual acquisition of general office skills and thus from one of the few promotional avenues open to secretarial staff.

Although word processing has as yet had less impact on the job content of personal secretaries (often due to the reluctance of managers to risk losing their status symbol), Bird's study for the Equal Opportunities Commission[21] found that the removal of much of their typing to a word-processing pool had left personal secretaries comparatively underemployed, and that there was an increasing tendency to use a single secretary as an administrative assistant shared between managers. Clearly, this breaks up the basis of the personal boss–secretary relationship referred to above with a consequent effect on the status of both manager and secretary.

A second significant consequence seems to be standardization that is experienced in two ways: standardization of the product, and the elimination of individual differences in execution. Because the productivity of word processors lies in their ability to store and reproduce commonly-used documents such as customer letters or reminders, thus eliminating the work of retyping, this seems to have resulted in many instances in word-processor operators being only given this sort of routine bulk repetitive work, with little original correspondence and without the varied mix of material of the typical office typist. This observation has been confirmed in a personal study of a word-processing pool in a Scottish local authority. Here the operators, while liking the speed and accuracy of the machines, complained that other departments were sending them all the bulky boring material such as committee minutes, because these always followed a standard pattern and were thus suitable for word processing.

Another reason for such standardization is that the word processor makes it possible for two or three operators to work on such long and bulky documents at the same time. This is only possible because the equipment formats all similar documents in the same way, thus eliminating any differences in approach to lay-out that different typists may have possessed. This must be seen initially as deskilling. Despite our earlier comment regarding the purely correspondence functions as being less skilled than the administrative functions, traditional typists do possess unique skills such as accuracy, speed, the ability to neatly and clearly lay out a variety of different types of document, centering, tabulation, correction, and spelling. The word processor undoubtedly does away with the requirement for all these except speed. There has also been a transfer of control over the job: whereas the traditional typist had to use personal judgment and experience to decide on how or in what order to tackle tasks, how fast to do them, or when to take a break, for the word processor many of these decisions are pre-made and there is more the feeling of being paced by the machine. This is especially so when the equipment is also recording the number of key-strokes per minute or the number of completed documents, or when linked to an audio bank of taped dictation. (Now go back and read our Prologue again!) The ability of word processors to monitor work performance also reduces the requirement for supervisory staff, thereby cutting out the other main avenue of promotion.

In the light of considerable evidence that the introduction of word processing is frequently accompanied by these alterations to the typist/secretary's job content, and the subsequent loss of the satisfaction that comes from the successful use of personal skills, the crucial question is whether there are likely to be any compensating satisfactions.

The evidence from a survey of word processing locations in Yorkshire[22] indicates that in the initial stages the attitudes of most office staff to new technology are usually favorable. This frequently has more to do with factors other than the equipment itself. For example, the combining of its introduction with a modernization or redesign of the office, or a financial bonus either negotiated by the union or offered as an inducement by management. More usually there is likely to be the sense of keeping up to date or "progressing" (based on those widespread social values we examined in Chapter 1) and perhaps the perceived chance to learn new skills and be relieved of boring tasks like correction.

In our local authority study, there was some evidence to support the idea that it was possible to gain new technology-related skills, in that the operators were able to modify aspects of the software and construct what were in effect "mini-programs" which enabled the main processing program to take short cuts when dealing with commonly occurring types of document. Some of the operators had become fairly proficient at this and there was considerable satisfaction at acquiring skills not specifically related to conventional typing. However, given the standardization of type of material dealt with, it seems likely that the construction of such miniprograms would be required in the early period of implementation only and might no longer be needed once the basic shortcuts had been worked out.

It must also be questioned how far this is likely to be a generally experienced situation. The word-processing pool in the local authority had been set up as a pilot project with a high level of input from the manufacturers to suit the needs of the operators. In contrast, most firms are likely to buy a word-processing package "off the peg," and most of these packages seem to make few demands on the operators other than to input the data. In the Yorkshire survey, three-fifths of the respondents felt that clerical workers had less control over their work after switching to new technology.[23]

To summarize this section, we have to note again that the acquisition of new skills can be a part of technological change (that is, there may well be no technological reason to explain a net deskilling), but that, on the basis of the limited evidence available, this seldom seems to happen. The use of new technology appears to increase the distinctions in the office between those who merely feed the computerized equipment with information and those who make decisions on the basis of that information, lending support to the "polarization of skills" model described earlier. In addition there seems the likelihood that this polarization will follow and exacerbate the traditional sexual division of labor in office work.[24]

EXPLANATIONS OF DESKILLING

Taking the evidence from our two examples of CNC machining and word processing we have noted that specialization, fragmentation, diminished control, standardization of product, and elimination of individual differences in job execution have all been observed to have happened following technological change, with only occasional evidence for the acquisition of new skills.

The big question is, why should this be so? Why should the introduction of a technology that clearly has the potential to take a lot of drudgery out of work, actually result in an apparent increase in job fragmentation, a reduction in variety of content and decrease in job satisfaction? For possible answers, we have to return to the distinction made between the "impact" view of technology, and the approach which treats technology as part of a social process.

If we hold the former view, then we are more likely to view these effects of job content as regrettable but inevitable: simply the unintended negative consequences of technological progress. In this view, any technology is going to have its effect on and demand changes in the organization, its management structure, the allocation and content of tasks, and the attitudes and experiences of the workforce. Even where the argument is pushed along slightly by suggesting that the organization should be seen as a "sociotechnical system" in which choices can be made, and that certain forms of organization might constitute a better "fit" with the technology than others, the technology is again treated as a given unchangeable variable and it is people who must be rearranged to fit around it more effectively.

The social process view directs our attention to the fact that the way technology is used and what it is used for are the result of a series of decisions made inside and outside the organization, and these decisions are frequently the result of interaction between groups (companies and their customers, companies and other companies, managers and workers, managers and shareholders) not all of whom will have the same priorities and interests. If we adopt this view, then the range of possible explanations increases. It both allows that choices are possible and also admits the possibility that managers may choose to adopt certain types of technology because of their organizational consequences rather than in spite of them. We also have to be prepared to consider the relative power positions of those with an interest in influencing the above decisions.

The most developed version of this view was advanced by the American Marxist writer (and former craftsman) Harry Braverman[25] who saw technological developments in modern capitalism as part of a continuing and direct attempt by management to increase their control over the process of production. The organizational techniques of F.W. Taylor's *Scientific Management*, which aimed to cut out every non-productive movement and moment from the workers' day, were, said Braverman, directly related to the development of assembly-line manufacture and similar technology that increased management's control by fragmenting whole jobs into smaller and smaller subtasks, and separating the "thinking" parts of a job from the "doing" parts of the job, removing the former to specialist groups of planners or incorporating them in the machinery itself so as to diminish the workers' ability to control the job. In short, in capitalist society deskilling was deliberate, not accidental.

The coming of new technology has given this line of argument a new relevance, and several studies have claimed to find evidence to support this view. Noble points out for example that there is nothing in CNC technology that makes it essential for programming and machine operation to be given to two separate groups: the technology merely makes it possible. He sees it as significant however that the pioneers of the use of NC machinery, General Electric, described NC as a management system rather than a technology of metal cutting. When he asked engineering managers in his survey why it was that the machinists could not operate the keyboard on the machine to edit the programs, after a few unconvincing answers the managers finally admitted that it was "because we don't want them to."[26]

Evidence that office automation too might be directed toward similar managerial goals is displayed in the following statement:

> The Taylorisation of the first factories . . . enabled the labour force to be controlled and was the necessary pre-requisite to the subsequent mechanisation and automation of the productive process. . . . Information technology is basically a technology of co-ordination and control of the labour force, the white collar workers, which Taylorian organisation does not cover.

These remarks are all the more significant in that they do not come from Braverman or a fellow Marxian writer but from Franco di Benedetti, Managing Director of Olivetti speaking in 1979 at a conference organized by the *Financial Times*.[27]

Although Braverman's approach usefully points us in the right direction, two criticisms can be made. First, it assumes that managers have carte blanche in deciding what will or will not be the way their workers relate to a given production process, thereby ignoring the possibility of reaction and resistance by the workers and their trade unions (see Chapter 4). Second, it assumes that every management policy is consciously directed toward depriving the workforce of any control they may have over the work, and therefore that technology that does deskill is deliberately introduced to do just that. However, managers have plenty of other things to worry about: the workforce is only one of the groups that they have to contend with. Therefore, whereas much technological change has resulted in the process of increased division of labor and deskilling, the causal chain may be more roundabout and indirect than a simple reading of Braverman suggests.

Out next case study illustrates some aspects of this by examining the ways in which the work content of draftspersons has changed with the introduction into the drawing office of Computer-Aided Drafting. CAD has the potential either to reintroduce elements of creativity into drafting or to intensify existing trends toward specialization and standardization. What factors influence the final decisions over how it is actually used?

Case Study: Computer-Aided Design

The drawing office occupies a key position in any manufacturing organization as the place where the conception and design of the end product get translated into specific manufacturing instructions, providing for example dimensions, materials, and often machining sequences through a combination of drawings and written instructions traditionally produced manually on a drawing board by an individual draftsperson. The work of the drawing office can therefore be divided into the creative or design side, where a concept or customer's request is turned into a practical reality; and the drafting or drawing side, which over the years has come to constitute the bulk of work done by the typical drawing-office worker and is usually far more routine and repetitive in nature.

Drawing office employees, as technical workers, have a special status in the organization, as by their social background and training and the necessity for regular contact and discussion with the manufacturing area, they bridge the traditional manual–white-collar gap between the shopfloor and the office.

Also, the nature of their work, though office-based, still very much falls into the classification of a "craft" occupation. Despite a continuing process of rationalization and specialization within the drawing office, it continues to contain most of the elements associated with craft work—skill, accuracy, responsibility, and a strong identification between the draftsperson and drawing, (indeed it is customary for each drawing to bear the draftsperson's signature at the bottom as "drawn by"). Draftspersons still take a pride in producing a "good drawing" that is clean, accurate, and clearly dimensioned, and can often recognize the work of their colleagues without reading the signature.

Because of this emphasis on quality of the work, time is frequently a secondary priority. Also, direct supervision and the measurement of output have both been fairly minimal in the drawing office, drawing office managers being able to rely on the "self-supervision" of their staff.

Into this environment has been introduced computer-aided design and drafting (CAD), where the draftsperson "draws" on a screen, using a variety of devices such as a light-pen or stylus and pad, rather than directly onto paper. Once completed, the drawing on screen can either be electronically stored by the computer, or printed into hard copy through a plotter. The design data base can also be used for future product modifications, or for further processes such as testing for stress performance.

Drawing-office management has a range of choices over how it will use CAD systems. First, CAD can be used interactively for creative design work, which could result in an improved product and thus in the longer term be beneficial to the organization as a whole. This, however, ties up expensive hardware as an "electronic pencil" used by only a few design staff and, given the nature of design, there may be long periods where there is no visible "output" from the CAD installations.

At the other end of the spectrum it can be used to facilitate the routine drafting and modification work that is more typical of the modern drawing office than it was 50 years ago. Rather than producing completely new drawings the average draftsperson today is more likely to be engaged in routine modifications to existing designs, or enlargements or detail work. At first glance, CAD appears to offer considerable advantages here, with the ability to perform much of this time-consuming work at the touch of a few keys. Use of CAD in this area is more likely to bring immediate cost savings to the drawing office, but conversely if the basic design is below optimum it could prove counterproductive in the long run to the organization as a whole.

On the other hand, it could free the drawing-office staff to spend more time assessing the quality of the drawing as a whole, thus perhaps raising the possibility of putting back into the draftsperson's work some of the creative design element which has been removed in the past through increasing specialization.

Conversely, because like all computer-based systems CAD is easily capable of monitoring individual output, the time taken per project and the number of mistakes made, it offers the potential for increased managerial control over the work process, and a corresponding diminution of the autonomous craft control over the job that the draftsperson to some extent still has.

It can be seen from this that the outcome of technical change on both the organization of the drawing office and the content of the job, by no means follows inevitably from the technical properties of CAD itself.

A survey of CAD-using firms in Scotland found that most drawing-office managers had rejected the use of CAD for design work as too expensive a way of tying up the equipment.[28] Because of the current rapid obsolescence rate of computer-based equipment, there was considerable pressure on managers to go for as rapid a rate of return on their investment as possible. Thus most CAD systems were being used for repetitive work, enlargements, and modifications.

Interviews with draftspersons working with CAD produced evidence that there had already been some loss of control over their work following the move from the drawing board, and that this seemed to be attributable to two processes, standardization and fragmentation. Standardization of the draftsperson's job arises out of two characteristics of CAD. First, when CAD is used in the way described above, the most effective way to make it pay is to build a "library" on computer file of standard components and subassemblies to be called up from memory and moved around in different configurations to obtain "new" drawings relatively speedily. Thus, there is pressure on CAD-using firms to standardize their products, or at least standardize the geometry and structure of basic components (size becomes irrelevant as the geometry can be redimensioned at the press of a key). This inevitably reduces the content variety of much of drawing-office work. Second, CAD systems reduce all drawing, labeling, and dimensioning to a standard format, irrespective of who is doing the drawing. This standard formatting reduces the draftsperson's traditional flexibility of approach, and means that different aspects of the drawing can be worked on simultaneously, increasing the practice of groups of drawing-office staff working on the same drawing, finally breaking the vestigial link between the draftperson and his or her drawing.

Whereas, at the time of the survey, most firms admitted to having no systematic method of measuring productivity in the drawing office, the majority believed that the combination of these trends towards standardization and the capacity of computers to record work would eventually lead to the development of a more formal system of work measurement.

However, the most visible effect of the introduction of CAD is what I have called "the fragmentation of social cohesion"[29] in the drawing office, based on the observation that the pressures on management to use CAD in the ways indicated above has a tendency to divide the drawing office in three ways: spatially, temporally, and socially.

Whereas traditional drawing-board work requires high and officially defined levels of natural and artificial lights, CAD screens (like most visual display units) have to be guarded against glare and light reflection. This, plus the requirement for what is usually a stand-alone computer driving the system to be housed in suitable air-conditioned surroundings, creates a tendency for the CAD installation to be located in a room separate from the main drawing office and that appears to be almost its direct opposite. Whereas the latter is a light, airy, sociable environment wherein draftspersons expect to walk around the boards and discuss each other's work, the CAD room is invariably dimly lit, frequently windowless, and contains usually only two to three draftspersons at any one time.

This division of CAD work from the main work of the drawing office is intensified by the emergence of a small group of regular CAD users from among the drawing-office staff, despite the fact that the company may have agreed to the union's demand to train all its members in CAD use and may even have started out with a policy of making the system a general resource to be used by all draftspersons. In practice, after a while the system is used by a few "dedicated" users only as management realizes that having the best people away from the work stations for any length of time inevitably requires a period of relearning when they return to CAD, leading to below-optimum operation. Where the union has been successful in negotiating a CAD-using premium (which admittedly is not often), CAD users have *de facto* become a new grade of draftspersons.

This tendency is given an added impetus by the almost universal move to introduce shift work into the computerized drawing office.

Computerization thereby becomes the instrument for making shift work no longer the experience only of shopfloor workers. The reason for shift work in the office is the same, however, in order to get maximum returns on expensive capital investment by running it as continuously as possible. Shift work in the drawing office is a thorny issue and has already created divisions between management and the union (who oppose it), the union and some of its members (who may want the extra money), and within the drawing-office staff. Sometimes it is only CAD users who work shifts, exacerbating the above tendencies to make them into a separate group.

Where CAD is subject to shift work, the work of drafting becomes divided by time. Due to the standard format already mentioned, work started by one draftsperson on the day shift can be continued by another at night, further weakening any sense of identification with the drawing.

The combined effect of all these changes is not lost on the draftspersons. Most of those surveyed feel that the traditionally important qualities of individual skill, accuracy, and experience had all become less important following the move to CAD. Although they agreed that it was easier to produce a good drawing (thus decreasing the requirement for skill and accuracy), and that time-consuming tasks like spotting and correcting errors were made easier, two-thirds said that once the initial "novelty" phase had passed they missed some aspects of traditional drawing board work, especially those of socializing among co-workers, identification with the drawing, and the general satisfaction of putting your name to a good piece of work. Furthermore, most expected that skills and satisfaction would continue to diminish.

These attitudes are the more surprising in that, unlike many clerical workers, draftspersons by the nature of their work are not apprehensive about technology. Oftentimes, their technical training included direct experience with shopfloor machinery. Many of them do not see "new" technology as new at all, and enjoy the initial challenge of operating the computerized systems and feeling that they are keeping up to date and equipping themselves with marketable skills. Yet this generally positive attitude to technology in the abstract is in many ways contradicted by their own personal work experience.

What this case confirms is that there is little that is technically inevitable about the effect that the process of computerization has on the quality of the work experience. As stated, CAD can be used in a variety of ways, some of them actually relying on and amplifying the creativity and skills of the draftsperson. However, the pressure on management to secure a competitive edge now, rather than in some distant time period, and to show some fairly immediate return for investment in CAD systems in the form of reduced project costs, has dictated that the systems are usually used to speed up the routine drafting end of the operation, further fragmenting the task of producing a drawing, introducing shift-work, and increasing standardization in design and approach to the work.

What is also important to note is first that the primary and immediate goal of management in introducing new technology was not to deskill the draftsperson's job but rather the usual priority of staying competitive, and second that management's ability to use the technology for managerial rather than technical purposes was curtailed by the existing bargaining power of the employees and their union. For example, managers agreed that CAD could (and one day probably would) be used for direct measurement of individual output, but admitted that they were not pushing for this as it was not worth the trouble and reaction they would get from the union.

THE WORKING ENVIRONMENT

As we noted at the start of this chapter, any assessment of supposed changes in the quality of work must examine both the content of the work and also the context within which it takes place. This in turn includes the immediate working environment and the degree to which this is experienced as pleasant, safe, stressful, or hazardous, as well as the wider industrial and economic environment, including the state of the labor and product markets, and the prevailing industrial relations practices in the organization.

The image projected of working with new technology is almost the antithesis of the popular picture of traditional industrialism—clean and tidy working conditions compared to the dirt and clutter of much industrial production, a technology with no dangerous moving parts compared to the traditional visible hazards of flywheels, drive-belts, cutters, and presses. It might seem strange therefore that much of the bargaining emphasis of trade unions in the industrial societies when bargaining over new technology has been concerned with health and safety.

Health and Safety

To summarize what has become a fairly complicated body of literature, we can say that health and safety concerns arising from new technology in the workplace fall into four major areas: (a) strain on the eyes and nervous system from concentrated work with screen-based equipment, (b) muscular strain from long periods of sedentary work and repeated actions mainly associated with keyboards, (c) the particular problems faced by pregnant women, and (d) what we might call general stress.

Eyesight

There have by now been many studies of operators of visual display units (VDUs or, in North America, VDTs), and they are virtually unanimous in reporting similar eyesight complaints, the most common being tenderness around the eye, loss of visual sharpness and focus, double vision, watering and ache, grittiness or dryness, burning and redness and seeing colored fringes.[30]

The problem with such a list is first that it includes a fairly wide range of discomforts, and second that they seldom occur in sufficient statistical concentrations as to provide an uncontestable causal link with the equipment.

Both of these points, however, are part of the much larger problem of accurately assessing occupational health hazards where these are of the nonvisible kind, especially where they affect the nervous and musculatory systems. We are all a little unique in our build and make-up: anybody putting their hand too close to a cross-cut saw will stand to lose a few fingers, four people staring at a terminal screen all day may each react in a different way. The first may feel no discomfort at all, the second complain of headaches, the third develop rashes to the face and neck, and the fourth suffer from blurred vision.

Therefore, there is often very little basis for comparison or the swapping of experience between workers, especially in the typical office where there may be only two or three VDUs at the most. There will be a tendency for the operator in some way to blame him- or herself, and thus many complaints are likely to be underreported. I have encountered this in my own research, where the VDU operator in an office that had officially reported no health and safety problems, would say in conversation, "Well I do get this backache by the end of the day, but that's just me—I'm a wee bit taller than most of the girls."

Although many of the smaller studies can, quite rightly, be criticized for not being scientific in their construction (e.g., not using control groups for comparison), nevertheless the widespread reporting of similar complaints must give pause for thought.

Despite one or two recorded instances of regular VDU operators developing cataracts in their mid-30s,[31] medical and optical opinion seems to be that VDU work does not cause permanent damage to the sight, although it may exacerbate eyesight problems that are already present but undetected. For most users, a period of rest from the screen is usually enough to rectify any complaints.[32]

However, what is equally clear is that such complaints and discomforts are far from uncommon, as expressed by this VDU operator:

> When you get home you feel tired and tense and irritable. All the girls here complain about headaches and waking up in the morning with puffy eyes. Sometimes when you're working you get very dizzy and have to have a break.[33]

The suggested reasons for this are almost as varied as the symptoms displayed. The early VDUs did not pay enough attention to levels of luminance, flicker-rate, and screen legibility, but the emergence of recognized industry standards does not seem to have abated the number of complaints recorded. Age is certainly a factor (people over 40 and 50 years old need up to 50% more light to read by), as are eyesight defects that had previously gone unreported or corrected. However, to allocate to these the total causal weight for eyesight problems among VDU workers is to return to the old fashioned "blame the worker's negligence" attitude to industrial health and safety.

An exacerbating factor is often the environment in which the equipment is situated. Offices built in the postwar period reflect the trend to the ever more "lighter and brighter" office—more big windows, more strip lighting, and these developments have created possibly the worst environment in which to locate screen-based equipment. The operator has to be able to clearly read and switch focus from copy, to keyboard, to screen, which requires rather special light levels to give both good legibility and contrast. Reflected glare on the screens from bad positioning opposite a window or directly beneath a light is still one of the most commonly reported grievances of VDU workers. In a survey of the use of 7,000 screens in over 200 workplaces, 63% of responses mentioned reflected glare,[34] almost exactly the same proportion found in another survey by the clerical union the Association of Professional, Executive, Clerical and Computer Staff (APEX).[35] Similarly the new equipment is not unfrequently dumped onto the existing standard office desk, whose shiny polished surface contributes still further to light reflection (and whose standard height has been designed for reading rather than repetitive keyboard use).

The major factor behind eye complaints would seem to be quite simply the length of unbroken time the worker is using the screen; we return to this when we look at the unions' responses.

Muscular Pain

The link between muscular pain and repetitive movements, especially those limited to one part of one side of the body, have long been known about in the context of industrial production; now, however, they are being observed in the office for the first time. "Repetitive strain injury" or tenosynovitis, has had previous incarnations as "washerwoman's arm," or "cotton-twister's cramp," and is currently appearing as "data processors' disease." Whatever the name, it is basically damage to the muscles and tendons arising from repetitive motions of the fingers, hands, and arms: if ignored or not given a chance of recovery through respite from the work, permanant damage can result. Less drastic but far more common are pains in the neck, shoulders, and arms, consistently reported in a significant minority of VDU workers. An American study matched VDU workers with controls of workers doing similar work in traditional ways and found a significantly higher level of problems relating to aches in the back, arms, neck, hands, and shoulders on the part of VDU workers.[36] The number of complaints and their location was more directly related to the type of work being done rather than any specific types of equipment, data-entry terminal operators being more prone than typists on word processors for example.

Potential Dangers in Pregnancy

Probably the most controvesial area of potential health hazards is the alleged danger to pregnant women and their babies. Since 1980, there have been at least 11 recorded clusters of pregnancy problems associated with VDU users in the United States and Canada, a major study in the United Kingdom, one in Australia, and one in Japan. The Canadian surveys found that although the number of pregnant women using VDUs was small, the percentage of those having subsequent problems (miscarriages or abnormal births) was high—running from 50–80%. With so many VDUs in use in North America, it has been said that these figures could be explained purely by chance although the usual rate for abnormalities in pregnancy is 10–15% of the relevant population. A large survey conducted by the Japanese General Council of Trade Unions surveyed 4,500 female VDU workers, 250 of whom became pregnant. Of these, 1 in 3 subsequently reported problems. Significantly, the chance of pregnancy problems seemed to increase with the amount of time spent on the screen: those pregnant women spending over 6 hours daily on the screen had a two-thirds chance of a problem, those spending from 3–4 hours had less than one in two, and for low-level users of less than 1 hour per day the numbers dropped to one in four.[37]

A British study of female staff of the Department of Health and Social Security offices at Runcorn on Merseyside identified 169 pregnancies occurring during the period 1974–1982. These were divided into "exposed pregnancies" (where women had worked with VDUs for at least 10 hours a week during the 3-month period before and after conception), and "unexposed pregnancies" which were used for comparison. Of the exposed pregnancies, 36% resulted in some form of problem whereas the percentage for the unexposed group was only 16%.[38]

These findings are still open to dispute, as are the suggested causes. The factor most concentrated on has been the level of both ionizing (e.g., X rays) and non-ionizing (e.g., radio microwaves) radiation emitted by VDUs. Several official bodies, such as the U.S. Food and Drug Administration, and Health and Welfare Canada, have declared that VDTs pose no radiation risk to the pregnant or non-pregnant alike, although unions like the British clerical union APEX take the view that such statements of emissions—being well below the permitted maximum—may induce a false sense of security in that such levels refer to the risks of fatal radiation or induced cancers. Quite simply, no one knows what the "acceptable" level is before biological damage is done to a fetus.[39] This uncertainty has not prevented one firm from attempting to cash in by promoting a "VDU Radiation Smock"! (As yet I have found no record of any woman sufficiently trusting in its abilities to wear one.)

If radiation is at fault then even solutions such as the negotiated transfer of pregnant women to nonscreen work become problematic because of the normal 3-month period before pregnancy can usually be confirmed (which is also the very period when a fetus is more vulnerable). Other suggested contributory factors to birth abnormalities, however, include poor posture from badly designed work stations and office furniture, or quite simply the heightened levels of stress recorded of VDU workers whether pregnant or not.

Stress

An American working women's organization has pointed out that three major myths about stress have to be demolished: (a) that it is the people with the greatest responsibility or decision-making to do who are most prone to stress, (b) that it is a personal state which people bring to work with them, or (c) that certain people are psychologically more prone to stress than others.[40] In fact, stress is now accepted as a legitimate occupational hazard which has its roots in both the content and the context of work.

Alarmingly, new technology, despite its public image, seems to be contributing to an increase in stress at work. The U.S. National Institute of Occupational Health and Safety found higher levels of stress among clerical VDU operators in an insurance company than in any other occupational group they had ever studied, including air traffic controllers.[41]

We have already encountered some potential causes of this, such as rigidly designed programs that give no opportunity for the operator to do anything but key in data or simple queries, and the consequent feeling of being "taken over" or "run" by the machine.

More generally, Cooley has observed about the computerization of intellectual work:

> When a human being interacts with a machine, the interaction is between two dialectical opposites. The human is slow, inconsistent, unreliable but highly creative, whereas the machine is fast, reliable but totally non-creative.[42]

If these two characteristics—the creative and the noncreative—are complimentary, then the advantages of computerization in augmenting the skills of the human are obvious. From the evidence so far, there are grounds for suspicion that this is not always the case and that, especially where the computerized system is used to monitor and measure the workrate of the operator, the result is a mental form of machine pacing where the continual attempt by a person to match the mechanical speed of operation induces cumulative levels of stress.

Health and the Organization

If we accept that at least some of the above areas of health and safety concern are direct consequences of current new technology usage, we must ask to what degree are these technologically inevitable, and to what degree are they determined by decisions taken over the organization of the work process.

Many of the complaints of glare, backache, noise from printers, and so on could be solved by comparatively simple rearrangements of the office (blinds on the windows, filters on the screens, different lighting) by spending a few extra dollars on properly adjustable seating and adjustable keyboards and screens that enable individual human differences to be taken into consideration. Although some firms have been prepared to do this (union pressure notwithstanding), other companies, having spent several thousand dollars on a word processing system, begrudge spending a few extra dollars on a footrest or new seat or document holder for the operator.

It is frequently overcost-consciousness that causes hazards. A few years ago there were headlines in the paper, "Robot kills man!" The first man to be killed by a robot had been a Japanese maintenance worker who had been crushed against a pillar when working inside a safety zone repairing the robot, which was accidentally activated. The Japanese management of the firm had crammed the robots into too confined a working space; precisely the reason robotics engineers are adamant that there must be a clear circle of space all around a robot, to prevent the above sort of incident.

Similarly it is the *way* new technology is being used that underlies much of the health and safety concern, rather than any necessary technically induced effects. Bad ergonomic design in the office is only showing up now, when it had not been particularly problematic before, because the patterns of work have changed. Instead of the typist making frequent trips to the filing cabinet, the office next door, or stopping to answer the phone we have seen that all too often he or she now sits in one position all day. It is specialization that is at work here, rather than new technology. Specialization means that the bad design of the chair now becomes a problem; it means that movements in the working day may be limited solely to keyboarding, producing the muscular aches and tensions described; it means that the attempt to maintain a high level of concentration and visual focus through the working day becomes increasingly stressful.

These work patterns, are not *technically* necessary—they are socially determined. The same can be said of the wider question of shift-working, now an increasing feature of clerical work.

Shift Working

The reason for shift-working has of course always been to maximize the return on investment in fixed capital, by running it as intensively as possible. As we have seen, because of the lack of capitalization in the office, shift-working has previously been a feature of blue-collar conditions of employment only.

This began to change with the introduction of the first mainframe computers. Because of their prodigious costs (and the advantages of off-peak use of communications systems), there were pressures to work them intensively and computer workers became used to working shifts. Now, with the computerization of the office, the pressures to extend the working day are extending into the hitherto "nine to five" world of the office. For some jobs such as draftspersons on CAD workstations, straight nightshifts are worked. In many offices evening "twilight" or "swing" shifts employ many women on a part-time basis at hours when their children can be looked after by others.

The phenomenon of shift-working by direct production workers has long been recognized as having several adverse physical and social consequences. Insomnia, stress, and high numbers of ulcers are well-known symptoms of shift-working, as is a high rate of marital breakdown and the breakup of a normal social life.

MANAGEMENT AND CHANGE

To put some of the issues discussed in this chapter into perspective we need to be aware of the wider situation in which new technology is being introduced in the late-twentieth century. Despite optimistic talk from national leaders, the labor markets in most industrial nations are depressed, the major economies are suffering sluggish rates of growth (except in a few high-tech centers), and capital has become even more concentrated and multinational in nature as fierce competition for static markets forces corporations into a wave of mergers and takeovers. These trends seem particularly noticeable looked at from the British experience, but are present in lesser degrees elsewhere in the industrial world. At the same time labor movements are losing both members and bargaining strength through a combination of the decline of traditional industries, a resurgence of non-union personnel policies, and (in the United Kingdom) government legislation.

These features present to industrial management an unfamiliar landscape, very different from that prevailing in the early postwar years, and many managers naturally feel that sticking to the old guide books and maps only serves to get them hopelessly lost. There is consequently a considerable degree of searching around going on for new paths out of the wilderness. New technology may be one way, new industrial relations practices another, and new methods of industrial organization a third. More usually, elements of all three are being tried simultaneously.

This demonstrates still further the limitations of simply attempting to look for the effects of new technology. If at the same time as new technology is being introduced there are significant departures from traditional industrial relations and personnel practices which themselves effect quality of working life, it is misleading to attribute causal significance to the technology alone when both technological and organizational changes may be responses to wider problems.

Child[43] has usefully identified four major routes in current management strategies to maintain competitiveness and profitability, all of which are closely interrelated with the introduction of new technology, and some of which we have already encountered.

1. *The elimination of direct labor*. New technology can be used in a variety of ways to continue the process of automation and to reduce the overall demand for labor through increased productivity, (in our terms through replacement and displacement effects).

2. *Contracting*. Contracting can take two forms. Whole areas of work (e.g., maintenance) may be contracted out rather than the organization continuing to keep a highly trained staff (e.g., maintenance engineers). This is facilitated by the fact that computers' ability for self-diagnosis reduces the amount of maintenance and the highly specialized maintenance that remains is often done by the system suppliers anyway. Secondly, there has been a resurgence of the old practice of outwork, this time in the form of computer-based "homeworking." Homeworking does have a pronounced effect on the way work is experienced and has been taken as a signpost to future patterns of work in the information society that is to come. (We shall examine it more fully in Chapter 6.)

3. *The degradation of work*. The continuation of the techniques systematized by F.W. Taylor: the separation of manual and mental work, fragmentation of tasks, division of labor, and so on. Whereas Braverman's view is that this is the dominant strategy guiding all man-

agement's actions, here it becomes only one in a choice of strategies and one which may not be best suited to prevailing conditions. Taylorism arose out of an assumption of long runs of mass-produced standard products as the industrial norm, in which the prime consideration was the reduction of the unit cost. If, as some economists have suggested, competitiveness in the present era is no longer solely in terms of price but rather in terms of quality, reliability, and design, then the rigid enforcement of Taylorist principles allied to some mystical sense of regaining managerial prerogatives may prove counterproductive. Given the contemporary need for product diversification and the shortened cycle of innovation, more flexible manufacturing methods and technologies are needed in which it becomes more important to enlist the cooperation and integration of the workforce. This situation might lead to a choice of the fourth option, below, and attempts at job redesign and participation (see Chapter 5).

4. *Polyvalence*. The increase in the flexibility of labor through a variety of practices including the breakdown of traditional demarcation lines, job enlargement and enrichment, and the creation of peripheral groups of workers. We have already seen how technology cuts right through many traditional job distinctions, even across the manual-labor–white-collar division. The increasing use of similar technology by hitherto discrete groups has facilitated the current trend towards labor flexibility within the organization, reflected in an increase in flexibility clauses in recent British collective agreements, including new technology agreements. This is allied to two further trends, that of training a core of regular workers with skills specific to that organization but not necessarily any one function within it thereby giving these workers a long-term identification with the company, and at the same time achieving flexibility of supply by relying more on temporary workers, agency workers, or groups with high labor turnover for a range of unskilled jobs such as basic assembly or clerical work. These developments are producing an effect on the way organizations relate to labor markets, which is very close to the Japanese model (see Chapter 5).

CONCLUSIONS

In summary, new technology has the potential either to enhance the skills of the operator and eliminate drudgery and a hazardous environment, or conversely to deskill and fragment work and contribute to stress. But the outcome is neither technologically inevitable nor organizationally inevitable. Although we have seen that hardware is often designed with little reference to the people who are to operate it, and that management do often choose to use new systems to enhance their control over the production process, it is too simplistic to attribute sole responsibility for a lowering of the quality of the work experience to either just the technology or the single-minded machinations of management. As some of the examples have shown, whether work is diminished or enhanced seems to depend on the interaction of several factors that include the assumptions incorporated into hardware design and the type of management strategy adopted, but also the nature of the product market and, last but not least, the nature and effectiveness of the trade union response. It is to this response that we now turn in Chapter 4.

DISCUSSION QUESTIONS

1. Is the amount of skill required for job performance determined by human, organizational, or technical factors?
2. Are there any grounds for expecting the level of skills in the workforce to rise with each generation of technological change?
3. What safeguards and practices could be introduced to minimize discomfort and injury arising from the regular use of IT office equipment?

REFERENCES

1. E. Braun & P. Senker, *Microelectronics and employment,* Manpower Services Commission, London (1982), p. 32.
2. Central Policy Review Staff, *Social and employment implications of microelectronics,* Her Majesty's Stationery Office, London (1978), p. 15.
3. R. Blauner, *Alienation and freedom: The factory worker and his industry,* University of Chicago Press, Chicago (1964).
4. T. Nichols & H. Beynon, *Living with capitalism: Class relations and the modern factory,* Routledge & Kegan Paul, London (1977).
5. J. Gershuny, *After industrial society: The emerging self-service economy,* Macmillan, London (1978), pp. 130–131.
6. H. Braverman, *Labor and monopoly capital: The degradation of labor in the 20th century,* Monthly Review Press, New York (1974), p. 427–430.
7. K. Kumar, *Prophecy and progress: The sociology of industrial and post-industrial society,* Penguin, Harmondsworth (1978), p. 211–219.

8. R. Grossman, Miss Micro, *New Internationalist, 150,* (1985), p. 12–13.
9. M. Duncan, *Microelectronics: Five areas of subordination,* in: L. Levidow and B. Young (eds.) *Science, technology, and the labour process,* CSE Books, London (1981), pp. 172–207.
10. Council for Science and Society, *New technology: Society, employment and skill— Report of a working party,* Author, London (1981).
11. B. Jones, Destruction or redistribution of engineering skills? The case of numerical control, in: S. Wood (ed.), *The degradation of work? Skill, de-skilling and the labour process,* (S. Wood, ed.), Hutchinson, London (1982), pp. 179–200.
12. Council for Science and Society, *New technology: Society, employment and skill— Report of a working party,* Author, London (1981), pp. 25–26.
13. B. Jones, Destruction or redistribution of engineering skills? The case of numerical control, in: S. Wood (ed.), *The degradation of work? Skill, de-skilling and the labour process,* (S. Wood, ed.), Hutchinson, London (1982).
14. D. Buchanan, *Canned cycles and dancing tools: Who's really in control of computer aided machining?,* Paper to Aston/UMIST conference on organization and control of the labor process, Manchester, (April, 1985).
15. D. Noble, Social choice in machine design: The case of automatically controlled machine tools, in: A. Zimbalist (ed.), *Case studies on the labour process,* (A. Zimbalist, ed.), Monthly Review Press, London (1979), pp. 18–50.
16. H. Braverman, *Labor and monopoly capital: The degradation of labor in the 20th century,* Monthly Review Press, New York (1974), p. 301.
17. H. Downing, Wordprocessors and the oppression of women, in: T. Forester (ed.), *The microelectronics revolution,* Basil Blackwell, Oxford (1980), pp. 275–287.
18. C. Gill, *Work, unemployment and the new technology,* Polity Press, Cambridge (1985), p. 44.
19. H. Downing, Wordprocessors and the oppression of women, in: T. Forester (ed.), *The microelectronics revolution,* Basil Blackwell, Oxford (1980), pp. 275–287.
20. Conference of Socialist Economists, *Microelectronics: Capitalist technology and the working class,* CSE Books, London (1980), pp. 44–45.
21. E. Bird, *Information technology in the office,* Equal Opportunities Commission, Manchester (1980).
22. U. Huws, *Your job in the eighties: A woman's guide to new technology,* Pluto, London (1982), p. 23.
23. U. Huws, *Your job in the eighties: A woman's guide to new technology,* Pluto, London (1982), p. 27.
24. C. Gill, *Work, unemployment and new technology,* Polity Press, Cambridge (1985), p. 48.
25. H. Braverman, *Labor and Monopoly Capital: The degradation of labor in the 20th century,* Monthly Review Press, New York (1974).
26. D. Noble, Social choice in machine design: The case of automatically controlled machine tools, in: A. Zimbalist (ed.), *Case studies on the labor process,* Monthly Review Press, London (1979), pp. 18–50.
27. U. Huws, *Your job in the eighties: A woman's guide to new technology,* Pluto, London (1982), p. 26.
28. C. Baldry & A. Connolly, Drawing the line: Computer-aided design and the organization of the drawing office, *New Technology, Work and Employment,* (1986), *1*(1), pp. 59–66.
29. C. Baldry & A. Connolly, Drawing the line: Computer-aided design and the orga-

nization of the drawing office, *New Technology, Work and Employment,* (1986), *1*(1), pp. 59–66.

30. Labour Research Department, *VDU's, Health, and Jobs,* Author, London (1985), pp. 4–5.

31. Association of Professional Executive Clerical, & Computer Staff, *New technology: A health and safety report,* Author, London (1985), p. 54.

32. Labour Research Department, *VDU's, Health, and Jobs,* Author, London (1985), p. 4.

33. H. Downing, Wordprocessors and the oppression of women, in: T. Forester (ed.), *The microelectronics revolution,* Basil Blackwell, Oxford (1980), pp. 275–287.

34. Labour Research Department, *VDU's, Health, and Jobs,* Author, London (1985), p. 5.

35. Association of Professional Executive Clerical, & Computer Staff, *New technology: A health and safety report,* Author, London (1985), p. 11.

36. Labour Research Department, *VDU's, Health, and Jobs,* Author, London (1985), p. 9.

37. Labor Research Department, *VDU's, Health, and Jobs,* Author, London (1985), pp. 16–18.

38. Labor Research Department, *VDU's, Health, and Jobs,* Author, London (1985), p. 18.

39. Association of Professional Executive Clerical, & Computer Staff, *New technology: A health and safety report,* Author, London (1985), p. 49.

40. Association of Professional Executive Clerical, & Computer Staff, *New technology: A health and safety report,* Author, London (1985), p. 57.

41. Association of Professional Executive Clerical, & Computer Staff, *New technology: A health and safety report,* Author, London (1985), p. 57.

42. M. Cooley, *Architect or bee: The human/technology relationship* (1st ed.), Langley Technical Services, Slough (1980), p. 15.

43. J. Child, Managerial strategies, new technology and the labor process, in: D. Knights, H. Willmott, & D. Collinson (eds.), *Job redesign: Critical perspectives on the labor process,* Gower, Aldershot (1985), pp. 107–141.

4

NEW TECHNOLOGY BARGAINING

THE INDUSTRIAL RELATIONS ENVIRONMENT

It is clear from the evidence of the previous chapters that new technology is *perceived* by those who have to work with it as having quite profound actual and potential consequences for their working lives, even if some of this potential has yet to be realized. For this reason, the trade unions have come to the fore in much of the copious amount of analysis and discussion of new technology that has taken place in the past few years.

Irrespective of nationality, the unions have seen technology as a development that simultaneously affects most of their major goals and raisons d'être: jobs, remuneration, hours of work, working conditions and occupational health, and perhaps the very existence of the unions in question.

The approaches adopted have ranged from the militant suspicion displayed by some European union movements, to the cautious welcome initially offered by American and Japanese unions. However, these reactions have all been accompanied by a wave of activity to win safeguards and securities for the areas most open to risk. In addition, there have been some prolonged work stoppages in Britain, America, and Germany over the introduction of particular items of new technology such as computer typesetting, strikes in several countries over such related issues as a shorter working week, and even such strikes as the 1984–1985 miners' dispute in the United Kingdom, apparently concerned with more traditional issues. These strikes have had the implications of new technology running through them as an underlying subplot.

Many people outside the often arcane world of industrial relations, reading of the latest strike over their breakfast tables, may feel inclined to wonder why there *should* be stoppages and disagreements over new technology. Whether we see these union reactions as either justified and understandable or as unwarranted obstructionism depends on the mental model we have of industrial relations and how it should operate. One view for example, sees the enterprise as a team, with each part of the team (management and workers) having their different roles to play. Management's job is to manage and make decisions in the organization's best interest. This unilateral exercise of managerial prerogative is the most effective way of getting the job done for the benefit of the whole team.

In this perspective, any instance of employee resistance to the introduction of new technology can appear as an ostrich-like head-in-the-sand approach that, by its senseless opposition to progress, is jeopardizing the employer's attempt to make the enterprise more successful.

This model of industrial relations, termed the *unitarist* model, has a long history and has had a resurgence of popularity among management in recent years. The trouble with this model as a basis for analyzing patterns of industrial-relations behavior is that it is extremely limited when it comes to explaining conflict.

Industrial conflict is common to industrial societies and displays the sort of patterns and regularities that social scientists find when seeking to understand any form of social action. For example, although industrial conflict may not always manifest itself in the same way, some societies such as Britain or Italy consistently display higher rates of strike action than, for example, Sweden or West Germany and some industries such as automobile assembly or mining have a regularly higher propensity for strike action than banking or retailing. In addition, the peaks and troughs of aggregate levels of strike action appear to be affected by movements in other economic variables, such as the rate of inflation or the level of unemployment.

If every industrial enterprise is a team in which all are on the same side, conflicts of interest must always be explained by temporary frictional causes (such as a breakdown in communication), or be attributed to external influences such as the work of agitators or even the intrusion of a trade union into the internal affairs of the company. These frictional or extraneous factors would create a far more random distribution to actions of manifest conflict than the examples above lead us to expect.

A more useful basis for trying to understand why there might be some instances of industrial conflict over the introduction of new technology is to accept that conflicts of interest continually arise in industrial employment. We are not saying here that there is no basis for cooperation or compromise in the enterprise (any more than we are saying that daily working life consists of incessant class warfare). It is rather that the employment relationship in a capitalist/free market/private enterprise-based economy is a more complex one than most of the ready formulas suggest. Some of the more basic features include:

1. Both employers and employees obtain the means of subsistence from the production of a product (a good or service) with exchange value, that is, one that can be solid. To this extent, the unitary view is correct: both management and workers have this common interest that provides the basis for day-to-day *cooperation.*

2. The employment relationship is a pecuniary one: The employee sells his or her labor power for a monetary reward. But whereas for the employer, wages are a cost of production and therefore in theory to be kept to a minimum, for the employee they are a means of subsistence (she or he has no other means) and therefore, in theory to be maximized. There is thus also present in the employment relationship an inherent *conflict* of interest.

3. In reality, these conflicting goals are constrained within narrower limits. Below a certain level of earnings, the employer will not be able to obtain the sort of labor required, above a certain level the employees run the risk of putting the firm out of business, thus losing the future means of subsistence. This still leaves a large area of potential debate over the appropriate wage for the perceived effort expended in the job by the employee.

4. The process of production (whether of a good or a service) inevitably involves a series of choices and decisions. Originally, all these lay with the employer by virtue of ownership of the means of production. The employment relationship has always to this extent been an *authority* relationship. What is made, how it is to be made, how many are to be made, are all largely predetermined before the

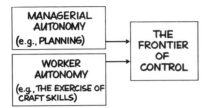

JOINT REGULATION VIA COLLECTIVE BARGAINING/
INDUSTRIAL DEMOCRACY
(e.g., OVER WAGE RATES, WORKING CONDITIONS.)

Figure 6. Regulation and control in the enterprise.

worker joins the firm, and the employer's authority is backed up by the sanction of being able to terminate the employment.

In reality, we find that employer-made rules are just one end of the spectrum of decision-making in the enterprise; at the other end, workforce members are frequently found to control parts of the production process themselves. In the middle is an area where neither party has autonomy of action, where decisions are made as an outcome of interaction between both parties. This has been termed the "frontier of control", and we may say that decisions made in this area take the form of joint regulation (see Figure 6).

There are thus potential conflicts of interest in two areas of the employment relationship, the control of the job and the rate for the job. More accurately, rate should be described as what seems an appropriate reward for what the employee perceives as his or her mental and physical effort (the so-called "effort bargain"). Therefore, from this perspective, the two areas of uncertainty are interconnected. The ability to control aspects of the job effectively controls the effort side of the wage–effort equation and to the extent that the employee has this control it is clearly to his or her material advantage; whereas if the employer has the control, the employer in turn is able to use it to attempt to maximize workers' efforts for a given wage rate.

The skeptic may say, if these conflicts of interest are always lurking below the surface, why is there not *more* conflict? Why do people not strike all the time? The answer is twofold. As point 1 (p. 87) suggests, people go to work to earn their daily bread: in this context perpetual conflict is in no one's best interest. Also, while the *terms* of bread-earning frequently need to be renegotiated, this in itself does not necessarily lead to overt conflict in the form of strikes or walkouts, because various institutional means have evolved to resolve these areas of uncertainty. We can identify the major means for this as follows.

The Components of Industrial Relations Systems

Individual Bargaining. Where unions are nonexistent or weak, such as in private sector white-collar employment, or newly industrializing societies like those of Southeast Asia, the only bargaining power possible over the terms and conditions of employment is likely to be between an individual employee and the company. Except for higher grade staff or perhaps where the company is very small, this personal bargaining will be fairly rare and is unlikely to yield much in the employee's favor. The frontier of control is also likely to be heavily skewed to reduce worker autonomy to a minimum.

Collective Bargaining. Collective bargaining becomes possible with the organization of employees into a trade union, in an attempt to minimize the power disparity in the employment relationship. Bargaining now takes place with the implicit possibility of sanctions being used on both sides, the threat of dismissal being matched by the threat of collective industrial action. The term *bargaining* includes both "official" bargaining through appointed trade union negotiators that culminates in a written agreement, and "unofficial" bargaining, when workplace representatives (such as shop stewards) or even groups of employees, negotiate an unwritten observance of a particular rate or working practice.

The structures of bargaining (and, it must be said, of patterns of industrial action when bargaining breaks down), frequently mirror the structures of trade union organization. The earliest unions were organizations of particular trades or crafts such as plasterers, iron-molders, or bookbinders, and this occupational basis for union organization is still found in Britain, the United States, Canada, and Australia. With technological change and the development of the division of labor, skills became less industry-specific and more transferable, and so these early occupational unions were joined by large general and industrial unions such as the Teamsters or the Transport and General Workers. In nations such as Sweden or West Germany, where the unions were forced to reorganize (either through the superior bargaining power of the employers or by a long period of attempted annihilation), a simpler and more logical industrial structure prevails with all workers in a given industry being organized into a single union. Elsewhere, as in France or Italy, the boundaries of division within the union movement are two-dimensional along both industrial and political or religious lines, whereas in Japan, the concept of "lifetime employment" in the large-company sector makes it logical for Japanese workers to be organized on an enterprise basis, so that Hitachi Company workers, wherever they work, will be members of the Hitachi Company Union Federation. It follows then that bargaining can take place at a variety of *levels*: at the level of the workgroup, at department or section level, at the level of the plant or factory, at company, industry, or even national level.

Industrial Democracy. In industrial democracy the attempt is to augment bargaining with structures that emphasize the bases of *joint* interest (e.g., the Works Councils in West Germany, worker-directors in Germany and Sweden, or more loosely structured *ad hoc* structures in individual firms like "user-involvement" committees). This approach necessarily requires both workforce and management to give up areas of autonomous control so that the area of joint regulation can be enlarged. Because of this relinquishment and certain historical factors, this approach has been less favored in Britain and the United States than in some other European countries. In Britain, for example, both management and unions have tended to view industrial democracy with some suspicion, tending to rely on more traditional collective bargaining.

State Regulation. Where collective bargaining has not developed to any great extent, perhaps because of employer hostility or the political position of the trade unions, then basic terms and conditions may be set by the state; a good example of this is offered by postwar France. Elsewhere state legislation may establish minimum criteria for working conditions (working hours, health and safety requirements, and so on).

These modes of decision-making are of course not discrete entities. Most industrial nations display combinations of some or all of these, and the precise mix (what for convenience we can call that country's industrial relations system) will obviously determine the character of any responses to the challenges of technological change.

These however are only the *structures* of industrial relations. How people behave within those structures can also largely be a consequence of prevailing attitudes and values, which will include the attitudes which employees bring to work (respect for authority, or a belief in the value of collective action), those which they learn at work (trust or suspicion), and the attitudes of management (insistence on the "right to manage" or paternalism). The combination of structures and attitudes helps to determine whether decisions made in these areas are the result of conflict, compromise, or cooperation.

UNCERTAINTIES AND STRATEGIES

We can say that the ways in which management and workforce cope with the stresses of technological change could depend on:

1. The structure of the industrial relations system in that particular country and the degree to which this is reflected in the industry concerned (the types of unions, density of union membership, whether the emphasis is on collective bargaining or on the industrial democracy, the levels at which bargaining usually takes place).
2. The existing boundaries of management and worker autonomy of control in the production process.
3. The cultural attitudes of the participants.
4. The economic climate, that is, the degree to which insecurity of employment and the lowering of pay horizons is exacerbated by a recession, or diminished by a boom.

Unions: Challenges and Responses

The structure of any trade union movement to a large extent mirrors the contours of the existing workforce, reflecting either the different trades and occupations, the individual industries, or even, as in the case of Japan, the major corporations. Therefore, technical change, which inevitably stands to alter the prevailing composition of the workforce, historically has presented trade unions with several major challenges. Following the themes discussed in Chapters 2 and 3, we can briefly identify these as concerning:

1. Payment and grading—in most cases past technological change has threatened to cheapen the work of specific groups (although

in some cases there may be an opportunity to bargain suc-
cessfully for greater rewards for scarce skills).
2. The threat to members' jobs—either through redundancy (or
natural wastage), or through the blurring of traditional demarcation lines so that work with the new technology can be
claimed as the prerogative of members of more than one union.
3. The continued existence of the union—threatened by the rapid
decline of specific trades or industries.

In addition, the experiences of new technology that other employees have already had may create additional uncertainties specific
to this particular era of technological change. These experiences are
likely to include:

4. A deterioration in working conditions, for example through new
health and safety hazards or the introduction of shiftwork.
5. A decline in job satisfaction and a threatened loss of job control.
6. A concern that members will have sufficient knowledge and
competency to work effectively with new equipment.

We can similarly identify four major ways of reacting to these
challenges, all of which have been suggested and tried in some measure
in relation to the latest challenge from new technology. A trade union
can:

1. Do nothing, either because it believes that the projected threats
will not materialize, or in the hope that eventually the stresses will sort
themselves out. It is not often that unions have adopted this course of
action through choice, but where the government of the day has re-
verted to laissez-faire policies and a reliance on the market mechanism
(as for example in the United States and Britain in the 1980's) then
there is likely to be a strong set of social values which sees any union
interference in the adoption of new technology as preventing the market
mechanism from working efficiently.

2. Accept the technology, but with as many safeguards and guarantees for its members as it can secure. Some of these will be achieved
through the methods of joint decision-making (collective bargaining,
industrial democracy, etc.), whereas others will be obtained through
the evolution of what the unions generally refer to as protective practices (and what conventional managerial texts usually refer to as re-
strictive practices), namely insistence on demarcation lines, the closed
or union shop, or entry through apprenticeship. These are all historically well-documented union strategies in the older industrial societies

such as Britain and America. Whether they can be relied on again in the face of the challenge of new technology depends very much on the speed at which it spreads. It may well be that new technology simultaneously affects many different areas of employment so rapidly (relatively speaking) that there is no time to work out lines of demarcation.

3. Resist the proposed changes and attempt to maintain the status quo. This is frequently referred to as "Luddism" after the textile machinery-breaking movement of early nineteenth-century Britain, with the implication that such obstructionism is short-sighted, irrational, bloody-mindedness. Yet this is to misunderstand the Luddites as much as the use of the label misunderstands the reasons for resistance to technological change in the 1980's. The Luddites were in fact rational workers who did not set out to break each and every textile frame, but specifically those belonging to employers who were using them to lower the price of the product below the customary level. At a time when the Combination Acts and a repressive government fearing a cross-Channel replay of the French Revolution had made forming a trade union an illegal act and the collective withdrawal of labor a criminal conspiracy, workers who saw their livelihoods threatened by new technology felt they had little alternative but to take that technology out of action; it was what Hobsbawm has called "collective bargaining by riot."[1]

By contrast today when many alternatives would appear to exist, most unions realize that it is unrealistic to expect support for a policy of total opposition, even if this is now expressed in the boycotting of the equipment rather than its destruction. Quite apart from the debilitating lure of handsome "golden handshakes" (or "golden parachutes"), many of those most affected by microelectronics are weakly unionized. Even where the union is well-established, there is now the strong possibility that if it takes too strong a stand, the employer will build a new plant using the new technology with non-union labor; the British print union SOGAT felt that this was so likely in the printing industry that it concluded that flat opposition to computerization would be a "rapid road to de-unionisation."[2]

Perhaps more importantly than any of these factors, several sectors of the workforce have already been made to realize that, by its nature, new technology makes many of the more traditional forms of resistance irrelevant. Shop stewards of the British draftsperson's and technicians' union, Technical Administrative and Supervisory Staff recounted how, when British Leyland announced in the early 1980's that their next model was going to be wholly designed in Japan, with the British factors almost solely limited to assembly, the union voted not to handle any of the drawings, data, calculations, or any of the other massive quantities of paperwork that have traditionally been necessary for the conception of a new car. They then discovered that this action was futile. New-technology-enabled management, by lifting the phone and dialing the computer code, to have immediate access to all the information it needed relayed by satellite from Japan.[3]

Management: Uncertainties and Strategies

In order that obstacles to harmonious change are not portrayed as emanating from one source only, it is necessary here similarly to itemize possible sources of managerial uncertainties when contemplating technical change. These are likely to include:

1. Costs versus benefits. Will the decision to invest in the equipment be rewarded in terms of the return on capital, and will this require altered work patterns, a reduced workforce or stabilized wage costs?
2. The possibility of workforce resistance, and protracted and costly delays in getting the system operational.
3. A concern that management will have sufficient knowledge and competency to manage the new system.
4. The fear of loss of control (with the switch to "invisible" electronic information, the visual monitoring of output becomes more difficult). Should work monitoring be incorporated into the system's programming or will that lead to workforce resistance (Point 2) mentioned above?

It can be seen that several of the items listed under both the union and management headings are essentially the same uncertainty looked at from opposite perspectives. If these potential areas of conflict can be regarded as inhibitors of change, there are also several factors shared by both sides that could be regarded as promoters of change, including, for example, the mutual vested interest in the economic health of the organization. We already noted that in the case of information technology both sides may share a generally positive attitude towards what is perceived to be technical progress, along with the desire to acquire new skills and new areas of knowledge.

Just as the unions were faced with a choice of responses, so management has a choice of introductory strategies. Among the most common have been:

1. To unilaterally introduce the system and associated working methods and use the state of the labor market to minimize any complaints.
2. To bring in the system and have a series of explanatory training sessions with employees after the event.
3. To negotiate a technology agreement with workforce representatives after system introduction.
4. To consult the workforce before introduction.
5. To negotiate an agreement with workforce representatives before introduction.

Extra money and/or reduced hours can be included as a "sweetener" in, or specifically excluded from, any one of these strategies.

THE CONTOURS OF BARGAINING

As stated, the employment relationship contains elements of both conflicting and mutual interest. The overall approach to collective bargaining by both management and unions varies significantly depending on which of these two characteristics each party chooses to emphasize.

Most collective bargaining arises out of, and emphasizes, the conflict of interests in employment, as each party seeks to redistribute the bargaining terms in their own favor. Such bargaining is often referred to as "zero-sum" bargaining—if one party wins, then the other necessarily loses, but the "sum" of their efforts represents no addition to the total rewards. In the language of the usual metaphor adopted in such circumstances, the cake that is being divided stays the same size, although the relative sizes of the slices may vary.

By contrast, under some circumstances it is the underlying mutuality of interest that is emphasized (thereby increasing the size of the cake to everyone's benefit). This cooperative approach is dubbed "positive-sum" bargaining. Although it is less common, it was hailed as the distinguishing feature of the early productivity bargains in the late 1960s before these decayed into a more traditional redistributive mode (although some critics claimed that such agreements represented a redistributive initiative on the part of management all along). On a larger scale, the national bargaining structures of Sweden and Norway are usually held up as working examples of the positive-sum approach and as an indicator that it can be economically very successful. It is clear that in its most developed form, such an approach becomes less a form of bargaining and more a form of industrial democracy.

It must be stressed that the above distinctions should not be adopted as an either/or model. Even conflictual bargaining is conducted in the knowledge that the parties have to work together once the dispute is settled and, conversely, areas of conflict are always there beneath the positive-sum surface, as evidenced by the recent breakdown of the Swedish centralized bargaining system under the dual strain of the recession and political conflict over the controversial wage-earner funds.

Just as approaches to bargaining may vary, the results of the bargaining process—the agreements—can also vary in appearance and function. The submerged part of the bargaining iceberg is informal, being conducted every day in thousands of workplaces, out of the spotlight of the news media, by workplace representatives on behalf of their members in that particular place of work. In this way individual and collective grievances such as disciplinary issues, someone feeling that they have been underpaid or changes in working practice, are resolved (e.g., appropriate rates negotiated for new or retimed jobs), and the working environment (e.g., heating, ventilation) maintained. The result of these activities are usually unwritten *ad hoc* agreements or contributions to the cumulative stock of custom and practice.

More formal negotiations, usually between trade union officials and company management or an employers' association, result in written agreements or contracts that in some societies (e.g., the United States, West Germany) are legally binding, whereas in others (Britain, France, Australia) they are not.

It is customary to distinguish between: (a) *substantive agreements* that set basic rates of pay, hours of work, holiday entitlements and other bread-and-butter issues, and (b) *procedural agreements* that mainly serve to lay down the rules of the game (how the parties will tackle frequently recurring and potentially conflictual situations such as redundancy, disciplinary matters, workplace grievances, or technical change). Procedural agreements specify the appropriate level of negotiation for each stage of the procedure, the time limits before the next stage has to be implemented, and what happens if there should be a failure to agree.

This condensed overview of some of the major features of collective bargaining has been necessary because new technology bargaining, while in its present form a new phenomenon, incorporates most of the above features to some degree.

The Principles of Technology Bargaining

The attitude of the British Trades Union Congress (TUC) towards new technology well exemplifies both the dilemma faced by the trade unions at the prospect of technological change and the degree to which they have accepted its inevitability. Because the British experience is particularly well-documented, we use it to examine the successes and failures of new-technology bargaining, with some comparisons with alternative strategies adopted elsewhere.

In its *Employment and Technology Report* (1979), the TUC General Council made it clear that it sees new technology as a neutral force whose positive benefits to industry and society will only be shared if stringent safeguards are secured against its potentially negative aspects:

> Whether technology will prove to be a friend or foe will depend not on the technology itself, but on its application and the policies adopted by government, trade unions and employers.[4]

To safeguard the workforce against these potentially negative effects, the report stressed that new technology agreements (NTAs) should as far as possibble cover the whole process of technological change from investment decision to working with the equipment, and to this end the report gives a detailed checklist of crucial principles for future negotiators. The most essential of these are that:

1. Change should always be by agreement: There should be full consultation before the decision to purchase has been made, and ideally a 'status quo' clause (i.e., a condition that things remain as they are until agreement has been reached), should be included in any NTA.
2. The British trade union structure makes multiunionism within a single plant a common phenomenon, and as we have seen new technology is no respecter of occupational demarcation lines. For this reason, the TUC recommendations lay great stress on the importance of joint union bargaining between the employer and representatives of all the unions in the plant wherever possible.

3. There should be a continuous provision of information from management to trade union representatives at every stage, linked to a regular process of consultation and discussion, and to assist this information flow, trade union representatives should build up their own expertise in technical areas.

4. The overall strategy of the union should be based on the objective of maintaining and improving employment and living standards and ensuring that new technology is associated with expanding job opportunities rather than a short-term policy of reducing the workforce to get a temporary increase in productivity. Unions should aim for no redundancies, should beware of the long-term effects of natural wastage, and should secure improvements in facilities for redeployment and relocation through improved training and financial assistance.

5. Bargaining by individual unions on working hours should be seen as part of the TUC's wider campaign for a reduction in the working week to 35 hours. Specific groups should use new technology bargaining to reduce their own hours of work, but the goal should be to use such breakthroughs as levers for progress for all workers. Wherever possible the reduction in working hours should include the reduction of systematic overtime.

6. Income levels should be maintained and improved, with emphasis on the additional skills required to operate the new equipment.

7. Procedures should be established that ensure that data acquired by computer-based systems is not used for the measurement of work performance. To this end, negotiators should seek involvement in system design.

8. Stringent standards of health and safety operation should be agreed, relating to adequate and regular breaks from the equipment, proper staffing levels, and regular maintenance.

9. There should be joint union–management study teams to review the progress of change and to speed up grievance procedures for issues arising out of the process of change.

The above list includes bargaining issues that are procedural (such as the disclosure of information and the need for joint-union bargaining) and many that are substantive (the maintenance of pay and jobs). Some of these may seem hopelessly optimistic, but it must be realized that the TUC saw NTAs as only one arm of a strategy for positive technological change that included continued government intervention in investment in a British-based microelectronics industry, and joint forward planning in areas of manufacturing and labor requirements. The demise of the Labour government in 1979 and its replacement by a government firmly committed to free-market forces effectively removed these other planks from the union's platform and forced them to attempt to secure all these objectives through new technology bargaining alone. With this in mind, we can take some of the major elements from the above list and as subsequently included by individual unions in their drafts of model NTAs for their own industries and attempt to assess how successful the British trade unions have been.

Procedural Objectives

The goal of gaining access to information at every stage of technological change and even being involved in system design is clearly quite a radical demand in that it pushes the "frontier of control" into areas that could be regarded as the heartland of managerial prerogative: investment decisions, economic versus social priorities, and so on.

Reviews of British new-technology bargaining so far[5,6,7,8] give little evidence of success in this area. The typical pattern seems to be that although management usually agrees to pass on about systems prior to introduction, this is still after the decision to purchase a particular system has been made, and the sort of information that would be necessary for any proper evaluation of an investment decision— production costs, transfer pricing practices, and other financial data— is scarcely ever made available. In other words, the frontier of control as yet seems little affected by new technology bargaining, the boundaries of managerial prerogative apparently being drawn in much the same place whether there has been new technology bargaining or not.

The practice of not informing trade unions and employees sufficiently in advance of the purchase of the equipment is not confined to Britain. In Australia, this practice earned management a rebuke from Justice Mary Gaudron, Deputy President of the Australian Conciliation and Arbitration Commission. Gaudron concluded that insistence on managerial prerogative to exclude workers from any involvement in decision-making relating to new technology not only contributed to industrial unrest surrounding its introduction, but posed the possibility that the equipment would not be optimally adapted either to the needs and skills of the workforce or the processes of production in the enterprise.[9]

There does not even appear to be any widespread acceptance of the principles of change by agreement only. Although there may often be an agreement to take any problem arising from the new equipment through the disputes procedure before full system implementation, the idea of mutual agreement as a prerequisite for introduction seems to be rarely achieved in British new-technology bargaining.

This limited success in establishing procedures for change which measure up to the original TUC guidelines may be partly due to the fragmented approach to technology bargaining taken by British unions. Despite the clear and widespread implications that new technology has for all unions, and the awareness that it has the potential to make irrelevant many traditional boundaries of identity between occupations or between manual and white-collar work, the evidence is that most new technology bargaining is very localized, usually involves only one union, and that most likely a white-collar union. Two-thirds of all monitored NTAs up to 1983 involved single plants or sites (even in multiplant firms) and four white-collar unions (APEX, ASTMS, TASS, and the National and Local Government Officers Association) accounted for most of the agreements signed. Even where multiunion agreements had been negotiated, investigation revealed many of these to concern only white-collar unions.[10]

This may be partly due to the fact that, unlike the office, technical change on the shop floor is not a new phenomenon. Manual unions have considerable experience of negotiating such change and often already possess procedural agreements or arrangements that they feel can cope with any new technological introductions.

Despite these limitations, most NTAs are procedural in composition. Whereas a large number of agreements combine procedural with some substantive elements, the same survey of NTAs found that purely substantive agreements, or specific *ad hoc* agreements relating to single items of technology only, together amounted to less than a third of all the agreements monitored.

The major substantive areas covered have been jobs, salary, and health and safety.

Job Security

Union objectives with regard to security of employment can be divided into short and long term, the short term relating to guarantees over the immediate consequences of the introduction of new technology. There are essentially three types of job-security clauses to be found in NTAs, diminishing in strength from that agreeing to "no job loss" at all, through "no redundancy," to the weakest, that of "no compulsory redundancy."

Although an agreement that there should be no redundancy sounds clear, it lacks the strength of a no-job-loss clause because it still allows for a gradual diminution of the labor force through natural wastage (or attrition). No compulsory redundancy merely adds the possibility of voluntary redundancies to such ways of diminishing the workforce. As we saw in Chapter 2, women's jobs are frequently in the forefront of transformation through new technology and women do have a higher rate of labor turnover than male members of the workforce because of wider social factors. For this reason, agreement to a no-redundancy clause is often an easy option for management, and such clauses do seem to be the most common job-security ingredients of current NTAs. The more rigorous "no job loss" is rarely achieved by the unions (and then mainly in local authorities whose political complexion makes them sympathetic to the unions' claims).

Although it could be argued that the extra cost of even a no-redundancy pledge would slow the rate of return on the investment and thus perhaps dissuade management from introducing new technology, the evidence seems to indicate that firms take such costs into their calculations before they start.

A pledge of no direct redundancy often costs management very little because they can always rely on natural wastage or early retirement to achieve the desired staff reductions, and because of the frequent difficulty of showing that staff reductions in one part of the plant are *directly* due to the introduction of new technology in another. Several unions have already found that NTAs in such circumstances offer relatively little protection should management declare that redundancies are due to more "traditional" reasons such as shrinking order books or foreign competition. Although the inability to secure "tough" clauses on job security has a lot to do with the unfavorable bargaining climate, it is also likely to be influenced by the fragmented single union pattern of bargaining, which inevitably creates a tendency both to put one's own members before the workforce as a whole, and to bargain for the security of the present job holders (i.e., current union members) rather than the jobs themselves.

The goal of long-term security has mainly been pursued through the wider campaign for a shorter working week. The TUC's goal of a

35-hour week is shared by most of the European trade union confederations together with individual unions in Canada and the United States. There is, however, some debate about how the time reductions should be obtained so as to secure the maximum spreading of the employment available—whether by taking half an hour or an hour from each working day, or by reducing the total number of journeys to work by aiming for a 4-day week. The Canadian postal union, CUPW, has calculated that shortening the working day by 1 hour to a 7-hour day would generate up to 2,700 positions in the postal service whereas a 4-day week would generate up to 3,700 full-time positions (or preserve those positions that would otherwise be threatened).[11] The difference is that the length of the day is reduced mainly through cutting the least productive time, thus requiring fewer replacements to be hired than would be the case with a 4-day week (which in another sense is an increase in paid holidays).

There are limits to the degree to which either of these options can offer a total solution to long-term employment problems. Jenkins and Sherman have argued that after a certain level, diminishing returns set in, so that whereas a 2% reduction in hours creates a 1% increase in jobs saved, a 16% unemployment rate requires a 27.5-hour week if it is to be eradicated. Nevertheless, several individual unions have long-term targets more ambitious than the TUC's 35 hours: the clerical union APEX aims for a 30-hour, 4-day working week,[12] whereas the Banking Insurance & Finance Union (BIFU), aims for a 4-day week of 28 hours total (but with the banks opening for six days a week).[13] Of course the unions' goal is to reduce hours with no loss of earnings, a demand based on the much vaunted improved productivity of the new technology. Management, naturally, sees this somewhat differently and the CBI has declared that shorter working hours for the same pay would simply be economic suicide in the present climate.

This points to an additional factor, namely the way in which the shortening of hours is obtained. If it is left to the bargaining abilities of individual unions, severe discrepancies (more severe than those which already exist) could result between the hours worked in the high-productivity new technology-using firms and those worked in the low-technology sector. Where basic hours are fixed for all employees by an external agency such as the state (which in France has reduced the national working week to 39 hours), then some smaller firms are likely to go under, adding of course to aggregate unemployment (or rather detracting from the aggregate number of jobs saved by the cut in hours).

Perhaps for these reasons, union success in reducing the working week, though not negligible, comes nowhere near the 35-hour target. In Britain, bargaining has obtained a 37-hour week for some workers, in Germany the very large and prolonged strike in 1984 by IG Metall for the 35-hour week (which the unions' Federation, the DGB, has made a clear part of its "Action Plan" for new technology) resulted only in a 38.5-hour week. In Sweden, night workers on continuous shifts work 36 hours. Sometimes the reduced time has been obtained by increasing the number of weeks of annual paid holiday.

In Britain, management often will readily agree to a vague commitment to a "gradual move towards a 35-hour week" being inserted in an NTA as a means to keep the union happy and give them something to show their members; although, as one manager commented, ". . . they know, and we know that there's not a cat in hell's chance of getting near it in the foreseeable future" (research interview, 1982).

Payment

The TUC recommended that unions use the acquisition of new skills as an argument for increased pay for their members using new technology. But this argument can prove to be a two-edged sword: as we have seen, there is a strong possibility that some jobs will be *de*-skilled as a result of computerization, and so the same logic would dictate that they correspondingly become cheapened. Most NTAs seek to prevent this with an agreement that no one shall be downgraded or suffer any loss of earnings as a direct result of new technology, but this only applied to the present job holders. In time, there is always the possibility that the jobs themselves will be regraded. For those unions who attempt to secure pay increases in return for operating the new equipment, there is a choice between seeking an increment for new technology operators only, or for using acceptance of the equipment as a bargaining lever to secure a package of improvements for all their members whether they use the equipment or not.

The determining factor seems to be the composition of the union membership itself. Those unions with an occupational base (craft unions such as those in printing, or "white-collar craft" unions such as drafters) are likely to try to secure an agreement on the specific equipment that is going to alter the work of their members (computerized typesetting or CAD). These agreements tend to be fairly substantive in content, aim for a new technology premium, and usually demand that all the membership be trained in operating the equipment. Such unions stand a reasonable chance of getting such guarantees because they have considerably more bargaining power through the control over the job resting in the skills of their members. They are quite able, if need be, to refuse to accept the new equipment, as we shall see in the case study of the printing industry. It may be however that such militancy represents the last fling of these particular skilled groups, as the equipment they are negotiating over largely removes the skill/control element of the job, and with it much of their bargaining power.

The problems facing general unions, especially those in the white-collar sector, are very different. Only some of their members in the workplace will be operating the equipment, and in addition levels of union membership are often much lower than for the craft or occupational-based unions who are likely to operate a closed shop. Under these circumstances, to go for a technology premium for operators only runs the double risk of creating an elite grade within their own membership or of seeing operating jobs being staffed by non-union personnel. Thus, such unions are more likely to negotiate general technology agreements, less related to specific items because so many different aspects of their members' work stand to be affected by new technology; such agreements will tend to have a high procedural content so that they act as framework agreements governing the introduction of any items of equipment, and increases in pay will be sought for the whole membership in the plant, whether they use the technology or not.

Payment increase can be handled in two ways: (a) a general hike in pay for everyone as an "entry fee" for management to get the equipment through the door and running, almost a compensation for accepting the technology "warts and all", or (b) an agreement that improvements in profitability will be shared equally among the workforce; in this way many NTAs become mini-productivity agreements. This kind of reasoning can again work both ways. Some companies have refused to sign NTAs because they claim that existing company agreements already state that the benefits from any investment by the company will be made available to the workforce (this of course conveniently ignores all the other aspects of new technology bargaining). In such circumstances, the union's ability to assess just what the material benefits of new technology have been and whether they have been distributed equitably is very limited.

The British clerical union APEX has actually made "output bargaining" part of its new technology strategy, and specifies that such bargaining should be kept separate from the annual wage and salary negotiations. The package they envisage, however, includes union involvement in system design, investment decisions and joint-union bargaining. If these elements are not forthcoming, and we have seen that in many companies they are not, then the NTA is likely to be reduced to the pattern described above.

Even where no extra payment is being sought for operating the new systems, new technology may still have an unsettling effect on existing payment structures by undermining the basis of existing job-evaluation schemes. For example, a scheme designed to measure and reward different elements in clerical work may not be suitable to re-grade staff whose work now requires familiarity with computerized processes. This has been true in areas of banking, where BIFU has claimed that it is resulting in a badly skewed and distorted payment structure. Regrading grievances are some of the more common issues arising after new technology has been introduced; although staff may have received an extra increment as part of the negotiated introduction package, they find they are still on the same grading even where the content of their work has changed significantly. This has been a frequent complaint of typists who have transferred to word processors.

Health and Safety

Health and safety clauses in NTAs vary enormously, reflecting the different degree of priority that individual unions accord to this area. Some are no more than vague agreements that adequate health and safety provisions will be made, whereas others are very lengthy and detailed, containing specific data on screen luminance and refresh rates, maximum hours for continuous screen work, length and frequency of break times, pledges on regular maintenance, and so on.

We saw in Chapter 3 that health and safety complaints relating to VDU operation do seem to be directly related to the length of time (especially unbroken time) that the operator is on the equipment. For this reason, most British NTAs have specified both a maximum amount of daily working time on VDUs and also an unbroken-time/rest-time ratio. A common example would be for the agreement to specify 4 hours maximum operation per day and a ratio of two hours to 20 minutes on and off the equipment. Negotiated maximum times however have ranged from 2 hours to 8 hours daily, while unbroken time can be from 45 minutes to 4 hours, and rest time (or more accurately, time performing other duties), can be from 10 to 30 minutes. The differences are accounted for not just by differences in the bargaining persuasiveness of the union, but also by the nature of the job. Jobs with a high visual demand or with a high repetitive content need more breaks than other types of work.

Because there are many instances where use of VDU's has exacerbated undetected eyesight defects, most NTAs signed by white-collar unions specify that regular VDU operators shall have periodic eye tests, most commonly either every 1 or 2 years or on request. In many cases the employer has agreed to pay all or the major part of the cost.

Several agreements have agreed to the transfer of those suffering from photosensitive epilepsy or of pregnant women away from VDU operation, but as we noted in Chapter 3, there remains the worry for women that any fetus could be damaged before pregnancy is confirmed.

No British unions have gone so far as the Italian unions to demand that automation be used to "improve health" through the automation of unhealthy jobs, such as paint-spraying and metal-stamping, represented in the 1977 agreement between FIAT and the Federation of Metal and Engineering Workers, but such a wider aim is more typical of a politically complexioned union movement.

Although there are some employers who maintain that health and safety fears or complaints are psychosomatic or unfounded, generally health and safety appears to be the area on which there is the most joint consultation and exchange of information. In part, this may be due to the desires of management to appear reasonable and of the union to demonstrate gains to its membership. It has also been suggested that health and safety provides a forum for raising more abstract fears and grievances for which conventional bargaining structures offer no outlet.

New Technology Bargaining So Far

After a flurry of bargaining in the early 1980s, the annual numbers of additional British NTAs have somewhat declined. It has been suggested that this early "Phase 1" will be followed by a second phase when many of the early NTAs will have to be returned to and renegotiated to give more emphasis to areas that have subsequently proved to be important, such as the principle of no prior change without mutual agreement.[14] It is also undoubtedly the case that should the bargaining climate swing more in the unions' favor, a significantly greater number of concessions would be sought.

However, at the end of Phase 1 of new technology bargaining in an industrial relations system of distributive bargaining such as Britain, it seems that it has seldom in either scope or content lived up to the principles established by the TUC or in subsequent individual unions' model agreements. In the first place, new technology bargaining remains a minority pursuit, the number of British agreements being quite small relative to the number of bargaining units. In a great many places, there is simply no union involvement in change at all, or it is coped with in a variety of informal ways. Many manual unions, after an initial period of concern, have let the topic drop as not really concerning them. Some shop stewards, seeing that NTAs have not prevented redundancies in major companies, have concluded that they may not be worth the paper they are written on, and have preferred to rely on traditional workplace militancy to protect their members' jobs.

In industries such as banking where levels of union membership are uneven, managements have refused to meet the unions' request for an agreement,[15] a resistance undoubtedly aided by the recession. It has been suggested that a pattern has emerged in some manufacturing companies whereby an attempt is made to impose "Japanese-style" levels of commitment on the workforce. After falling demand has led to significant redundancies, management offers new technology as a "take it or leave it" package that will ensure the survival of the company. The core of remaining employees are offered greater job security and conditions in return for their acceptance of the equipment and a pledge not to challenge any further pruning of the workforce that may prove necessary.[16] Where technology has been introduced unilaterally by management however, it is often the case that the ensuing problems of payment structure have proved so complex that they have been forced to go back to the union and commence negotiations. Where NTAs do exist they are, as we have seen, mainly localized single-union agreements that do not depart from existing structures of bargaining.

The content of agreements has undoubtedly been influenced by the economic climate. In an economy displaying consistently high levels of unemployment, it is rare that NTAs have obtained cast-iron guarantees over job security, although direct redundancies arising from technical change have probably been minimized. Although there has been some reduction in the hours of work, extra payment for new responsibilities has only sometimes been won, and health and safety standards show considerable variation. Despite these limitations, the unions are in agreement that conditions for their members would have given far more cause for concern if there had been no agreements at all.

In one sample, 23% of responses said that union pressure had delayed or prevented a loss of jobs, prevention mainly being through internal redeployment.[17] It is also clear from the replies that where an NTA had been signed, the workers were more likely to have received some sort of compensation for the introduction of the equipment (that is not necessarily the same thing as a wage or salary increase as this compensation may be in the form of a once-and-for-all payment).

Significant omissions from many NTAs are any signs of an ability to affect either the skill content or the satisfaction in the job, or indeed to bargain on control issues at all, however for many clerical workers the health and safety concessions won through new technology bargaining represent the first time that they have had a say in determining their working environment.

Despite the unions' efforts to claim extra responsibilities for their members, it would seem that downgrading is the fate of many jobs transformed by new technology. Several agreements preserve the grading of the current job holders, implying that the job will be downgraded when they are replaced; other agreements actually permit downgrading.

Although many agreements state that the new technology will not be used to monitor or measure work rates, many unions recognize that this is unrealistic in that measuring and monitoring are among the things that a computer does best—it is in the very nature of the beast. Work measurement, especially in the office, they secretly admit, will come in time.

Some unions, notably APEX, are making a brave effort to secure a satisfactory content for their members' jobs by advocating union involvement in job redesign. We look at this in more detail in Chapter 5.

So the unions have concentrated on the traditional triad of jobs, pay and conditions, and health and safety. There is a certain grim logic in this set of priorities in that unless the union preserves its member's job, that member is going to find issues such as job satisfaction supremely irrelevant. One writer has concluded that what the unions have achieved in these basic areas represents the minimal conditions for the conclusion of any agreement, in that if they did not get *some* sort of pledge on redundancy or security of earnings, they would not be doing the job they were established to do.[18]

Trade unions in Britain seem to face an uphill task in obtaining even these minimal conditions. There has been a high incidence of new technology being introduced by management with no negotiation at all,[19] or negotiations taking place as a response by the unions after the equipment had been introduced.[20] This attitude to bargaining and change is not limited to management in the private sector. U.K. government departments have apparently been instructed not to give any undertakings that they will only proceed on technology introduction after joint agreement, and specifically told not to enter into any agreements which undermine "the right to implement projects without union agreement".[21]

What this evidence and previous examples demonstrate is that seldom is new technology an issue on its *own*. In some industries, such as coal-mining, it may be introduced in the context of a long-term contraction and program of pit or plant closures; in others, it may be linked to job evaluation and regrading, or a change of product. This simply reinforces the point that we cannot understand the effects of new technology without understanding the environment in which it is being used. Also, as stated, new technology will be introduced using established bargaining procedures that may be found wanting in their ability to cope with the stresses of technical change.

As Moore and Levie have pointed out,[22] the experience of negotiating new technology does not just support the need for a good NTA or a technology representative as *the* solution: it can question the adequacy of existing bargaining arrangements and the capability of the unions' response. NTA's are at most a start, seldom an end in themselves.

CONFLICT

With such an emphasis being placed by the unions on the desirability of collective bargaining over the terms of introduction and operation of new technology, it might be asked how it is that there have still occurred several major instances of industrial action and overt conflict over these issues: strikes, refusal to work with the new equipment, and withdrawal of cooperation.

In the first place, of course, all bargaining is carried out within a framework in which each side possesses implicit, often unstated sanctions. For the trade unions, these have traditionally been based on their ability to collectively withdraw their members' labor, and on the employer's side on the ability to terminate the employment relationship. In recent years, this last sanction has increasingly taken the form of the threat of total closure of a productive location unless cooperation is reached.

Every process of bargaining, no matter how sophisticated in structure, always gets to the point where it either can "deliver the goods" or it cannot. It is where it cannot, where neither party can get enough out of the proceedings for a satisfactory compromise, that these hitherto unstated sanctions become a distinct possibility.

In other instances, refusal to use the equipment may be used as a spur to management to get some negotiations under way, as graphically described by a workplace representative of the drafters' union, TASS:

> Now we have been to the company and we have said to them: "What are the implications on the workforce? What are the operating times? How many operators are going to be required to use it? Who is going to analyze the information that comes off the computer? What facilities have you made available for education and retraining of the people employed?" And they have sat back and said, "We don't know yet." And that is not good enough. So we have said to them, "Until you put it in writing and you can give us firm guarantees that the only people working that equipment when it is introduced will be the people at present employed at the plant, that they are going to receive the correct remuneration for operating the equipment, and that there will be no job loss, then you are not having that machine on site. We are not going to use it."[23]

This idea that industrial conflict occurs when bargaining breaks down in a failure to agree (or, as above, does not get started quickly enough), constitutes the conventional analysis of conflict; it suggests that the major way of diminishing conflict is to improve the bargaining mechanism. Thus, in the above case, had there been an existing procedural agreement on technology that specified prior consultation and exchange of information, the boycotting of the equipment would probably have been unnecessary.

However, this view of conflict although partially true is not totally adequate, as it assumes that every aspect of the employment relationship is negotiable and open to the bargaining process. From the evidence on the narrow spread of NTAs so far, it is clear that this is certainly not always the case with respect to decisions over technological investment. Child, for example, has described how banking management have almost universally defined such decisions as an essential area of managerial prerogative (see Figure 6) and refused union requests to enter into bargaining over them despite the banking union's commitment to securing NTAs.[24]

Elsewhere it may be that it is the trade union that feels the potential implications of the technology for its members' jobs and its own survival are so great that it is not prepared to see these as negotiable or to bargain over the terms of its own demise. Thus, where bargaining is not possible (just as was the case with the Luddites), then collective action may seem the only way to enforce a solution. It is usual to see such action being at the initiative of the workforce, but it is becoming less unusual in recent years for employers to actually close the plant and, using the flexibility of new technology, open up somewhere else (often, as we shall see, with non-union, or another union's labor).

We have spoken up to now of the workforce and the union as if they were synonymous. Although this is useful shorthand when considering official bargaining policies and practices, when looking at the actual reactions to technical change, we have to make a distinction between the two.

First, members may be either less well-informed, or generally less suspicious of the technology than the union leadership. This again seems to be the case in banking, where the employees in many cases have welcomed the technology for relieving them of many of the more boring tasks.[25] For this reason (plus others such as the uneven spread of membership among the workforce), the refusal of management to bargain has provoked very little support for the bank union's appeal for action.

In another situation it may be the members, through their direct experience of how change is affecting them, who may be more aware of the dangers and less willing to wait for the official processes of negotiation to take their course, or who are less prepared to agree to the general principle of the acceptance of new technology which perhaps the union is negotiating for the whole industry. There is no doubt that the onus of pinpointing where change is occurring and of initiating negotiations usually falls on the shop stewards or workplace representatives. It is now not uncommon for large well-organized workplaces to have joint-union new technology monitoring committees specifically to exchange information about what is going on in different parts of the enterprise.

Finally, of course, there is the fact that many of the employees most directly affected by new technology are not members of any union. It might be imagined that they therefore have no means of reacting to changes in their working environment but this is never strictly true; it is more accurate to say that their forms of action will be more restricted.

We have here to distinguish between collective forms and individual forms of industrial action that employees can use as a response to those negative aspects of their work for which bargaining seems to offer no solution. Collective action includes striking, slow-down, working to rule, banning overtime, and boycotting equipment, all of which require some form of organization to be effective. Individual courses of action however include sabotage (see the Prologue), absenteeism, a myriad individual ways of working without enthusiasm, and finally leaving the job altogether (reflected in high rates of labor turnover). The distinction is that, whereas union members could respond by adopting any one of these forms of action, nonmembers are really restricted to the latter category.

Downing, describing the work situation of traditional women clerical workers, says that collective action and union activity were often seen as a particularly male sphere of activity, but that the women had evolved a considerable "culture of opposition" whereby they could use a range of elements in the unstructured nature of their work to 'create space' away from the job of typing, such as going to another office to consult a file, taking a long time to make telephone calls, dropping paper clips in the typewriter well and being unable to do anything until repairs were made.[26] Downing quite rightly points out that all these forms of action are likely to become impossible with the advent of new technology, especially as we have seen that one of the express purposes of computerized office systems is to eliminate the unstructured element from office work.

If this does happen, it does not necessarily mean that such employees will henceforth happily spend all their time solely in productive activity. Employees do not react only to new technology, this "culture of resistance" was already present in the *pre*automated office. If the causes of discontent remain but the means of individual amelioration are removed, then one possibility could be an increase in unionization among such employees so as to make possible the collective redress of grievances.

There has been some debate as to the likely impact of computerization on the overall propensity for industrial action as a whole. There seem to be two possibilities: either new technology, through its enormous flexibility, offers employers a far greater number of ways to by-pass such traditional forms of industrial action as localized withdrawals of labor, or it gives small groups of workers in key positions in computer systems enormous power to exert leverage on management.

We have already mentioned one example of the first instance, the case of the Austin Rover technicians who found themselves temporarily powerless to prevent design data being transmitted to management electronically. More striking examples are provided by the printing industry wherein electronic transmission of text means that actual printing no longer has to be done in the same geographical location as text input, thereby by-passing the traditional areas of control by the printing unions. Such action is even more likely when the firm in question is a multinational corporation (MNC), the new technology having enormously increased the ability of MNCs to multisource their operations around the world. Thus Rolls Royce threatened the union at its Sunderland plant that they would fly N/C tapes to Rolls Royce Miami, if the unions did not agree to the proposals for working with new technology.[27]

It is also undoubtedly true however that certain groups of workers find their bargaining leverage significantly enhanced through new technology. In one respect, this is merely a continuation of a trend that has long been evident as the different sectors of industrial economies become more interdependent. In the nineteenth century, with its localized production and regional markets, no single group of workers could be said to "hold the country to ransom." Today, if the fulminations of politicians are to be believed, a whole range of groups, some of them quite small, are capable of doing just that. Also, the more the actions of employees in the production process become dictated by the nature of the fixed capital they work with, in both their content and their sequence, so it is likely, as Cooley has argued, that any deviation from this sequence comes to have a disproportionately disruptive effect.[28]

If these are already established trends in industrialized economies, it is clear that computerization, which both increases sectoral interdependence and makes routine many hitherto unstructured jobs, could greatly add to the potential for employee leverage in certain crucial occupations.

It may be, to anticipate for a moment the futurology theme of Chapter 3, that bargaining in the future will depend not so much on the ability to prevent or interrupt production, but rather the interruption of the information flow. Some indication of the degree to which the wielders of political power have already realized this is given in the American study that attempted to list the consequences for a society in the event of the total withdrawal of computer facilities (as might occur through some sort of national strike action). In order, these were given as: loss of military security, disruption of communications, loss of internal security, the disruption of industry, and social disruption (transfer payments of all kinds).[29] With this in mind, it comes as little surprise to find that significant effort is being directed towards "taming" (or where possible, eliminating), trade unionism in the new key sectors such as electronics and software production.

Demarcation

Historically, technological change has often been accompanied by disputes over job demarcation or "who does what" issues. They are more likely to be a recurrent feature of those trade union movements, like that of Britain, whose origins lie in the organization of specific occupations or trades. In the past, such disputes have been a feature of industrial relations in certain craft-based industries such as ship-building (e.g., in the transition from rivetted to welded hulls) and in printing (with the move to offset and lithographic methods).

Although they are commonly referred to as union versus union disputes, this is misleading, as ultimately the dispute is always with the originator of change, the management, who so often in the past took such decisions with no consultation or consideration of the implications for the workforce.

It was to prevent the repetition of such conflicts that the TUC urged that new-technology bargaining should wherever possible be on a joint-union basis, representing all unions in a given enterprise who were likely to be affected by the change. We have seen already that the degree to which this recommendation was put into practice has been minimal, and therefore some demarcation issues have become inevitable.

There are two ways in which new technology can affect the established boundaries of bargaining units—by eroding recognizable job demarcation lines within the enterprise and by its ability to reach outside the walls of the enterprise into areas that were hitherto completely autonomous.

One of the most frequent examples of erosion has been caused by the impact of CNC machine tools on skilled engineering machinists. The control of the machine by computer has, as we have already seen, threatened to reduce the skilled machinist (who in Britain is a member of the AUEW/ES), to what is virtually a glorified machine minder while the conceptual calculations on how the job is to be tackled have been removed to the Programming Department, whose technicians in Britain often belong to a different union, the draftspersons' union, TASS. (Until recently this was also a section of the AUEW but this has not prevented instances of less than cooperative relationships between themselves and the engineering section.)

Because it is possible to correct or edit out the bugs in the programs actually on the machines, this has frequently created contention over who it is that should do this. The AUEW/ES policy is to keep as much work on the shop floor as possible, and many of their members have demystified the world of computers very rapidly by picking up the ability to edit programs from watching the technicians. Understandably, the TASS part-programmers (who may eventually be bypassed anyway when the move to full CAD/CAM becomes operational—see Figure 1), claim it as their responsibility.

It is only rarely that this issue has been resolved through joint-union bargaining prior to the introduction of the machines. A more usual outcome is an *ad hoc* settlement for one workplace only, often following some sort of action or threatened action, some settlements giving the work to the machinists, some to the technicians. A typical compromise found in one electronics firm in Scotland allowed ES section members to do all the alterations concerning machine feeds and cutting speeds, while TASS members did those alterations concerning the geometry of the product.

An example of the second sort of change, that which takes the work of members of the bargaining unit outside the enterprise, is to be found in the growing link between banking and retailing already examined in Chapter 2. Although full EFT-based shopping is still at the experimental stage, several banks have started installing electronic cash-points in stores and supermarkets, leading the banking union, BIFU, to complain that the machines were being refilled not by banking staff but by shop workers.

The Effects on Union Organization

If individual unions are worried about the number of jobs available to their members following the introduction of new technology, the unions as a whole on one hand are confronted by falling membership brought about by continuously high levels of unemployment and the steady contraction of the older heavily unionized industries, while on the other hand the new growth sectors in microelectronics are remaining impervious to union organization. This is worrying enough for British unions who, for the most part, have been steadily growing since the war; for American unions who have been on the defensive for many years, the threat posed by the current restructuring is even greater.

The last time the unions faced such a challenge was the growth of the new light and electrical-engineering and chemical-based industries of the 1930s. These new companies with their high use of assembly-line techniques required labor-force skills that were not industry-specific and so were readily transferable from, for example, confectionary to radio-assembly. This posed a problem for the older unions who, through mergers and expansions, tried to expand their original occupational basis to include the new industries, while large gains were made by the newer general unions who were ideally suited to organize such forms of labor. There were severe ''poaching'' problems in several industries as different unions tried to oust each other as the bargaining agent for this or that particular group of workers. The situation finally led the TUC at its 1939 Congress at Bridlington to establish what eventually came to be referred to as the Bridlington Rules, whereby it was agreed that no union should recruit any group of workers in which another TUC-affiliated union was already acting as a bargaining agent, and that any membership dispute between two unions would be referred to the TUC for settlement.

This procedure has been adhered to in spirit, if not in the actual letter, for most of the British postwar period. Similar developments in the United States led initially to severe rivalry between the newer industrial unions and their federation, the CIO, and the older occupational unions of the AFL, which was finally resolved by the formation of the AFL/CIO in 1955.

The current restructuring, of which microelectronics and computerization form integral features, again present the unions with major problems. Several of the newer firms have taken advantage of the economic climate to exclude the unions entirely from their operations.

The pacesetter here is definitely the colossus of the computer world, IBM, who has always maintained a non-union organization, taking a somewhat unitary one-big-team approach to personnel relations, and this model has recently been strengthened by the example of Japanese corporations operating in Britain.

Unable to rely on British unions for the same sort of committed cooperation they can expect from Japanese enterprise unions, the Japanese companies have either opted for a no-union policy or have managed to sign no-strike agreements with single unions in return for recognizing that union as the sole bargaining agent.

The levels of unionization among microelectronics firms are thus generally low. At the Nippon Electrical Company factory at Livingstone New Town, for example, the company recruited its whole workforce entirely from school with no previous industrial experience. This mirrored recruitment and training patterns in Japan, but it also ensured that the workers had no trade union experience, and no union has been recognized. The situation is more pronounced in the software companies; many of these are small and work on a personal relationship basis. The unions, for their part, feel it important that they recruit horizontally into the software houses, from where the packages that control their work operations come and where control over the job is now largely determined.

As we have already mentioned, new technology has made easier the task of those employers intent on "union busting" or at least dismantling closed shops which have served to maintain high manning levels. In the British printing industry the attempts of Mr. Eddie Shah to run a non-union advertising paper, the *Stockport Messenger*, led to a prolonged and bitter dispute in 1983 in which the print unions were supported by many others and which culminated in mass demonstrations and confrontation with the police in front of the Warrington printworks.

One union in particular in Britain, the EETPTU, has taken a very different line from that of other TUC-affiliated unions. Established in the electronics industry, it has presented itself to Japanese and American management setting up in Britain as the union of moderation and responsibility. In return for recognition as the sole bargaining agent it has signed no-strike agreements such as the 1981 Toshiba Agreement, which have been watched with some interest by management elsewhere. As we shall see in the following section, the union was also prepared to offer itself as the new printing union to those printing employers who are contemplating ridding themselves of the old print unions and setting up computerized operations.

The unions are reacting to this double threat of changing demarcation lines and an overall loss of members by hastening into a flurry of mergers. Some of these make no technical sense, but simply represent a small financially weak union looking for added strength in the arms of a big brother. Other attempts at merger, such as the proposal between the National Graphical Association and the National Union of Journalists (see p. 120), had a distinct logic but came to nothing.

In the long run, more profound changes are likely to include the erosion of the staff/blue-collar distinction. Terminals are now used on the shop floor and in the office, office work is becoming routinized and machine-paced, and as we saw earlier, the same work can be fought over between members of both manual and white-collar unions. Eventually the lead given by the Swedish unions will be followed and all workers will be on staff status with the same hours, holidays, and general conditions.

From the factors we have examined so far, we could predict that the strongest opposition to new technology is likely to occur in areas where the changes in production techniques are so total as to completely by-pass a specific group of workers, where there are few opportunities for these employees to be transferred into other areas of the enterprise, where the trade unions are based on these specific occupations with strong demarcation boundaries and where there has been a strong tradition of control over the production process.

The newspaper printing industry seems to fit this description perfectly.

CASE STUDY: NEWSPAPER PRINTING

The production of newspapers is currently undergoing dramatic technical changes condensed into a very short period of time. Prior to computerization the process of production had altered relatively little in a century. The introduction of offset and litho methods in the 1960s had changed the way the type produced a printed page but had not altered the basic division of labor between composition and press work (performed by skilled manual workers), editorial work and journalism, and semi-skilled manual and clerical work (see Figure 7).

In Britain, following a series of union mergers, these three areas were, by the 1980s, organized by three major unions—the National Graphical Association, the National Union of Journalists, and the Society of Graphical and Allied Trades (SOGAT). In addition, electrical and maintenance workers were organized by the electrician's union, the EETPU, whose numbers in the industry were growing as the technology became more complex.

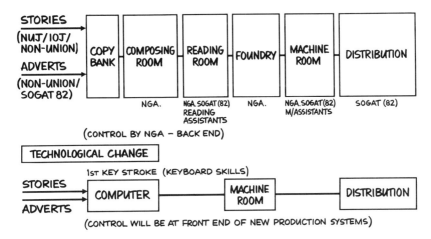

Figure 7. Change in the printing industry.

When computerization was added to the photographic techniques used in Webb offset, the first major challenges to this structure began. Typesetting was now done on a computer keyboard instead of a linotype setter and the computer justified the material, stored it, and transmitted it to a photosetter.

Given the powerful editing and correction facilities of computers, the next logical step was direct entry in which keying in material and photosetting were combined and where the initial keyboard input was done directly by journalists. Direct entry could be used not only for journalistic copy but also for that originating out-of-house such as advertising, sporting results, and weather forecasts, which could be keyed in by clerical staff in the tele-ad and related departments.

Thus, as Figure 7 shows, direct entry (or "front-end systems" as they are sometimes referred to), especially when combined with other technical developments such as facsimile transmission, spells the potential demise of a particular category of skilled workers, the composing-room staff, and threatens to deplete their union, the NGA. The strategies which the union has adopted to cope with this have run almost the whole gamut of those available.

An initial attempt through the TUC Printing Industry Committee to get an agreement between the major unions resulted in the 1976 Program for Action which was however rejected by the print unions' membership despite the recommendations of their officials. From then on, the development of newspaper technology has been marked by frequent conflicts between union and management and union and union.

An early casualty was the *Times* in London where an attempt to impose a direct-entry system resulted in an eleven-month strike and lockout in 1978–1979, at the end of which management gave up the idea. Many national and provincial newspapers settled for a halfway system of dual-keystroking in which journalists originated and edited material but the final input was done by composing-room staff (retitled keyboard operators).

Even this compromise reduced composing-room staff by 50% and contained several areas of waning influence for those NGA members remaining. The move from linotype to qwerty-style keyboards immediately reduced the specific skills necessary for composing work and made much of the traditional apprenticeship irrelevant.[30] Also, the increased flexibility demanded by management of composing-room staff undermined the autonomy of individual union chapels (branches) based on the traditional division of tasks.

The next response of the craft union was to seek a merger with one of the other printing unions. Initial talks with the journalists (the obvious choice given the NGA's policy of retaining control over keystroking) eventually broke down after profound disagreements over the nature and structure of internal union democracy. Other exploratory talks were started with SOGAT and with other communications unions outside the newspaper industry,[31] but these were rudely interrupted by a series of initiatives in the early 1980s taken by provincial newspapers to go for pure direct entry systems, which threw the NGA into a series of conflictual situations.

In some instances, the NGA were successful in getting some of their members retrained as subeditors (thereby causing a walk-out by the journalists). In another case, they agreed to single-keystroking in the tele-ad department if they organized the tele-ad staff into the NGA (putting SOGAT on the defensive). Elsewhere industrial action against the new systems led to NGA staff being sacked and non-union labor being hired.

It is the threat of non-union labor, now that the specific skills of the composing room are gone, that lurks unseen but ever present behind all these disputes. The British printing unions are worried by the example of the United States, where the Newspaper Guild lost its closed-shop position at the *Washington Post* following a strike over staffing levels on new printing equipment, and where new publications such as

USA Today are produced by a handful of non-union labor on new technology and transmitted by satellite to 26 separate printing sites.[32]

Such drastic results are slightly more expensive for management to obtain in Britain as British national newspapers rely less on external agencies for their news copy and more on their own journalists, and as well as the fact that the distribution of the papers is heavily unionized. Nevertheless, in 1987, one or two proprietors made a bid to follow the American example.

Mr. Rupert Murdoch's News International (owners of the prestigious *Times* and the unprestigious but mass-circulation *Sun*) are currently attempting to forestall competition from non-unionized newcomers into the industry by breaking the position of the printing unions in a strategy that combines most of the above techniques. During a fairly blatantly engineered dispute that brought the NGA and SOGAT out in joint action, production was shifted from Fleet Street, traditional home of British newspapers, to a preprepared new technology site in London's dockland. Here, behind barbed wire and searchlights, the papers were produced not by print union members (2,000 of whom have been declared sacked) but by members of the electricians' union, the EETPTU, who had been trained to operate the new equipment and distribution was undertaken by a transport company part-owned by Mr. Murdoch. This resulted in an extremely protracted and violent dispute which included mass picketing of the plant for a period of over a year, the use of the British Government's new union legislation by the employers to secure termination of the action by the print unions, crippling financial penalties imposed by courts on the unions when they refused, the threat of expulsion of the EETPTU from the TUC, and finally an admission by the unions of defeat.

The above account is drawn from the experience of the British printing industry, but is well paralleled elsewhere. Mention has already been made of some developments in the USA; in West Germany in 1977–1978, after a bitter dispute the Printing and Paper Workers Union, got an agreement that design and correcting work in computerized typesetting should only be done by skilled printworkers for the first 8 years after the installation of new technology. Those displaced have to be retrained for new jobs within the same plant (or helped to relocate) with a 6-year guarantee of no loss of earnings.[33]

It is also important to realize that we have only looked at the effects on one particular technological change within the newspaper industry. In addition, the industry as a whole is facing a challenge from new forms of news and information transmission such as Viewdata systems, which could replace many of the functions currently performed by papers (especially local papers) such as classified advertisements.[34]

It might seem from the above examples that in seeking to alter the production process in an industry like printing, managers have little option but to confront the structure of union organization head on, and the workforce has little option but to engage in battle or fatalistically acquiesce to a technological inevitability. We shall however, return to the printing industry in Chapter 5 to examine the possibilities of non-conflictual technological change.

DISCUSSION QUESTIONS

1. Why does the introduction of information technology into the workplace sometimes result in industrial conflict, and what steps could be taken by both sides to minimize this?
2. What should be the main priorities of (a) management and (b) the unions when contemplating technological change?
3. Evaluate the success of new technology bargaining in protecting the interests of trade union members in the face of technological change.

REFERENCES

1. E. Hobsbawm, The machine breakers, *Labouring men,* Weidenfeld & Nicholson, London (1964), pp. 5–22.
2. SOGAT '82 *New technology: The American experience,* SOGAT '82, Hadleigh (1985), p. 3.
3. National Computing Centre & AUEW/TASS, *Computer technology and employment,* NCC Publications, Manchester (1979), p. 32.
4. Trades Union Congress, *Employment and technology,* TUC, London (1979), p. 7.
5. T. Manwaring, The trade union responses to new technology, *Industrial Relations Journal, 12*(4), 1981, pp. 7–25.
6. B. James, *The trade union response to new technology,* in: D.L. Bosworth (ed.), *The employment consequences of technological change* Macmillan, London (1983).
7. N. Ash, Bargaining and technological change, *WEA studies for trade unionists* (Vol. 10 (37)), Workers Educational Association, London (1984).
8. R. Williams & F. Steward, Technology agreements in Great Britain: A survey 1977–1983, *Industrial Relations Journal, 16*(3), 1985, pp. 58–73.
9. ATU Handbook, *Technology and union response,* Trade Union Information & Research Centre, Sydney (1984).
10. R. Williams & F. Steward, Technology agreements in Great Britain: A survey 1977–1983, *Industrial Relations Journal, 16*(3), 1985, pp. 58–73.

11. Canadian Union of Postal Workers, *Reduced working time now*, Author, Ottawa (1984).

12. Association of Professional, Executive, Clerical, & Computer Staff, *Automation and the office worker*, Author, London (1980), p. 52.

13. Banking, Insurance, & Finance Union, *New technology in banking, insurance and finance*, Author, London (1982).

14. N. Ash, Bargaining and technological change, *WEA studies for trade unionists*, (Vol. *10*(37)), Workers Educational Association, London (1984).

15. J. Child & M. Tarbuck, The introduction of new technologies: Managerial initiative and union response in British banks, *Industrial Relations Journal, 16*(3), 1985, p. 29–33.

16. N. Ash, Bargaining and technological change, *WEA studies for trade unionists* (Vol. 19(37)), Workers Educational Association, London (1984).

17. Labour Research Department, *VDUs, Health and Jobs*, LRD, London (1985), p. 50.

18. B. James, The trade union response to new technology, in: D.L. Bosworth (ed.), *The employment consequences of technological change*, Macmillan, London (1983).

19. Joint Forum of Combine Committees, *The control of new technology: Trade union strategies in the workplace*, Author, London (1982).

20. R. Moore & H. Levie, The impact of new technology in trade union organisation, *Social Change and Technology in Europe Information Bulletin No 8*, Commission of the European Community, Brussels (1982)

21. M. Cooley, *The new technology: Social impacts and human-centred alternatives*, Technology Policy Group Occasional Paper 4, Open University, Milton Keynes (1983).

22. R. Moore & H. Levie, The impact of new technology on trade union organisation, *Social Change and Technology in Europe Information Bulletin No 8*, Commission of the European Community, Brussels (1982), p. 38.

23. National Computing Centre and AEUW/TASS, *Computer technology and employment*, NCC Publications, Manchester (1979), p. 37.

24. J. Child & M. Tarbuck, The introduction of new technologies: Managerial initiative and union response in British banks, *Industrial Relations Journal, 16*(3), 1985, pp. 19–33.

25. J. Child & M. Tarbuck, The introduction of new technologies: Managerial initiative and union response in British Banks, *Industrial Relations Journal, 16*(3), 1985, pp. 19–33.

26. H. Downing, Word processors and the oppression of women, in: T. Forester (ed.), *The microelectronics revolution*, Basil Blackwell, Oxford (1980), pp. 275–287.

27. Joint Forum of Combine Committees, *The control of new technology: Trade union strategies in the workplace,* Author, London (1982), p. 9.

28. M. Cooley, *Architect or bee?: The human–technology relationship* (2nd. ed.), Hogarth Press, London (1987), p. 110.

29. I. Barron & R. Curnow, *The future with microelectronics,* Open University Press, Milton Keynes (1979), pp. 26–27.

30. R. Martin, New technology and industrial relations in Fleet Street, in: M. Warner (ed.), *Microprocessors, manpower and society*, Gower, Aldershot (1984), pp. 240–252.

31. J. Gennard & S. Dunn, The impact of new technology on the structure and orga-

nisation of craft unions in the printing industry, *British Journal of Industrial Relations,* 21(i) 1983, pp. 17–32.

32. Society of Graphical and Allied Trades, *New technology: The American experience,* Author, Hadleigh (1985).
33. European Trade Union Institute, *Negotiating technological change,* Author, Brussels (1982), pp. 44–45.
34. National Graphical Association, *Printing and change,* Author, Bedford (no date).

5

ALTERNATIVE APPROACHES TO CHANGE

THE SEARCH FOR ALTERNATIVES

In international comparisons of levels of industrial conflict and "strike-proneness," Britain usually appears towards the middle, displaying neither the high propensity for strikes of the Italians nor the very low levels of the Swedes. However, during problem periods in British industrial relations, it is not surprising that British management have often looked at other nations with envy and attempted to discern a key ingredient in their industrial relations systems that could be adapted to the British context and contribute to a more harmonious relationship between managers and employees.

The introduction of new technology has promoted a new spate of this sort of speculation, as some sections of management search for a better way of negotiating technological change than the reliance on traditional collective bargaining that we examined in Chapter 4.

In this chapter, we analyze the examples offered by three societies often looked to for a model of industrial relations harmony, West Germany, Scandinavia, and Japan, and then at an alternative approach increasingly being tried in the United Kingdom, that of participative job redesign. Nevertheless, we take a fairly critical approach, showing that there is no ideal route to change that does not involve confronting some conflicts of interest and priority, and that most attempts to overcome this pose both advantages and drawbacks.

West Germany

The system of securing agreement on wages and conditions of work in West Germany has a dual structure. Although individual German workers may be union members and may have union stewards ("trustmen") within the plant, the union is prevented from having any recognized existence for bargaining within the enterprise and instead usually bargains with employers' associations at regional or industry levels. Because agreements at this level (which are legally binding) can only concern basic rates and conditions for the industry as a whole, there obviously needs to be some mechanism whereby these negotiated conditions can be applied and modified to suit the local situation in each company.

This mechanism is provided by West Germany's highly structured system of industrial democracy, and in particular the works council that in most workplaces of reasonable size represents all manual and staff employees, whether union members or not. The works council is legally prevented from calling strike action and thus has no sanction of collective action to back up its opinion. What it does have however, are legal rights to information, consultation, and codetermination over a wide range of issues that elsewhere are covered by collective bargaining or unilateral managerial decision-making.

For example, since the Works Constitution Act of 1972, the employer must give the works council prior information of structural changes in the size of the plant, technical equipment, working methods and personnel recruitment, training, and transfer requirements. The works council must be consulted by management on matters relating to changes in work processes and available jobs, staffing and dismissals, and in areas such as the organization of working hours and breaks, methods of wage payment, the allocation of annual leave, health and safety, and the measurement of work performance, the council has legal rights of codetermination of these issues with management. In other words, management is unable to intake unilateral decisions in these areas.

Some writers have alleged that the works councils, when added to the West German practice of codetermination by worker directors on the supervisory boards of companies, constitute such a well-developed system of industrial democracy that it must be seen as representing almost an evolutionary advance in the development of industrial relations.[1] The clear advantage over traditional collective bargaining with its assumption of divergent interests is said to be evidenced in West Germany's consistently low strike record. The cooperative approach incorporated in the practice of industrial democracy is also held to be consistent with a societal preference for harmony arising out of an historical experience that has made the West German people suspicious or wary of any overt appeal to conflictual interests.

New technology has been seen by the West German labor movement as part of the wider issue of "rationalization." This became increasingly important in the 1970s, and it was clearly the works councils who were in the best position to negotiate adaptation to the changes that it brought. Their response was initially ambivalent (unlike the unions they have no existence outside the company) and so, in their role as joint party to much of the regular decision making in the company they supported rationalization in principle as "securing the future of the firm through better products and improved productivity" which in the long run they hoped would secure jobs. On the other hand as part of their function of representing the interests in the workforce they were concerned to protect those directly involved from any possible negative consequences, and so sought to make rationalization "socially bearable."

The dual strategy of the labor movement was therefore to rely on the unions to bargain at a level above that of the individual company on the length of the working week and general guarantees on employment, much in the manner of a general "framework" NTA such as we examined in Chapter 4. Meanwhile, at plant and company level the works councils would attempt to control the planning, introduction, and use of new technology through codetermination.

How successful have they been so far? A case study of the Volkswagen plant at Wolfsburg suggests that from a trade union point of view codetermination in West Germany has not been noticeably more successful than collective bargaining in Britain. The authors conclude that, despite the fact that the works council in Volkswagen has secured wider powers of codetermination than the legal minima, the influence of the workforce on the formulation of goals and decisions relating to rationalization seems to have been limited.[2] This is even more surprising in the case of Volkswagen, because the company is unusual in West Germany in negotiating company agreements with the union (because of its high level of state ownership Volkswagen has never been part of the employers' association).

The agreement between the works council and management at Volkswagen seems fairly typical of the sort of guarantees that have been achieved over rationalization in most West German plants of any significant size: it was agreed that existing rights and status of employees would be protected, reductions in staffing would not take place through compulsory redundancy and that any short-term or seasonal fluctuations in demand would not result in fluctuations in the demand for labor.

At first, in the early 1970s, such guarantees of employment security were in practice only possible because of the bufferlike effect of the presence (especially in auto plants) of considerable numbers of *Gastarbeiters* (foreign migrant workers) from Turkey, Yugoslavia, and other areas marginal to the European labor market. Such workers were under stronger pressures to take voluntary severance than the indigenous German workers, and a substantial reduction in the labor force took place as many of these "guest workers" went home. As the potential for this diminished, greater emphasis was laid on the principle of early retirement. At Volkswagen after 1975 under the so-called "59 rule," it was possible for workers to retire a year early (the retirement age already being lower in West Germany than the United Kingdom), and the company paid the difference between the state unemployment pay and their previous wage. Even when the West German government changed the rules to prevent this, the scheme was so popular that the company continued to pay unemployment pay out of its own funds, as a cheaper way of reducing the workforce than actually declaring redundancies (the cost of redundancy payments being higher for a firm in West Germany than in the United Kingdom). The early retirement age was later dropped to 58.

There is little in the previous case that could not be found in the average British NTA. Conversely, just as NTAs were limited in their ability to affect job content, so it is for the works council. There were only a few cases where the Volkswagen council had succeeded in getting its ideas and demands on job design and training measures accepted by management and similar limitations have been remarked on by the union I.G. Metall in the case of Opel.[3]

The main reason for this is that on the issue of job content, the works council cannot codetermine but only advise, following consultation by management. Similarly, they will be informed of, but cannot usually prevent, the introduction of the new productive systems (although the Volkswagen works council held up the introduction of CAD system for 1.5 years). Their aim has therefore been to attempt to secure an agreement that this information will be made available at the earliest possible stage so that they are in a better position to negotiate over the social or personnel consequences. To this end, the Volkswagen works council established its own technical advisory committee, recruited from all the relevant departments within the company, to provide the council with the necessary technical expertise, help it evaluate company proposals and formulate alternatives.

However, the German employers have fiercely resisted any attempt to expand the scope of local agreements on new technology made with the works councils, and have sought to retain as managerial prerogative all decisions over the actual selection and implementation of systems. Thus, in 1978, the BDA (the German employers confederation) included new technology as part of its so-called "taboo-catalogue" of areas over which management must retain control.[4]

Does this mean that there are no essential differences between a system where plant-level problems of technological change are decided through industrial democracy and one where they are decided through collective bargaining? One survey of existing research has concluded that one significant difference, especially apparent in the case of an industry like automobile assembly where cyclical fluctuations in demand are common, is that in America (and United Kingdom) these fluctuations are more likely to be met by adjusting the total number of workers employed, whereas in West Germany the adjustment will be through the total number of hours worked.[5]

This points to one important area of influence by the works councils, the fact that they do have codetermination rights over the "effort" side of the wage-effort bargain: working hours, the number of holidays, and other types of annual leave. So at Volkswagen, to spread the volume of work in the face of the increased productivity of the new systems, they negotiated additional work breaks and extended educational and recreational leave periods.

The other significant difference is that collective bargaining remains essentially a voluntary activity, and we noted in Chapter 4 that new technology bargaining presently remains limited to a number of key firms and sectors, many companies having refused to undertake it. In contrast, the rights of the works council, though limited and not backed by the sanction of collective action, are laid down in statute, thus ensuring that the council must be involved in the taking of certain kinds of decisions, such as those pertaining to working conditions. Therefore, most local agreements between work councils and management are really a consolidation of the legal rights of the councils to information, consultation, and codetermination as these are applied specifically to rationalization. The same reliance on the law is shown in the health and safety guidelines relating to new technology: most of these are close adaptations of the guides issued by the Industrial Injuries Institute, a joint union–employer body that the 1973 Work Safety Act gave the right to introduce regulations on specific areas of health and safety.

There does seem to be some evidence that, by causing the employer to consider the social consequences of technological change before embarking on new investment programs, the works councils may have minimized the number of compulsory redundancies and ameliorated the impact on the workforce.[6]

However, it should be noted that measures such as early retirement, and the guarantee that if a job is downgraded the earnings and status of the worker are maintained for specified periods, only secure the position of the individual worker and do not tackle the problem of the overall level of employment in the future or the eventual downgrading or deskilling of jobs once the present incumbents leave them.

The longer term effects at a wider level than that of the individual company have been the concern of the trade unions. In 1983, the Federal Republic's largest union, I. G. Metall, called one of the largest strikes in the postwar period in all the metal-working industries in an (unsuccessful) attempt to gain the 35-hour week as part of the unions' long-term action plan on new technology. The recognition of the limitations of the works council in directing the course of technical change has increased the amount of cooperation between the two "arms" of the German labor movement. Most large works councils now contain a high percentage of union activists, and the unions often take up the local demands of the works council and press them in a more general form in their negotiations with the employers' association. The European Trade Union Institute concludes its review of the West German approach to negotiating change by saying:

> It is clear that important as rights to information and consultation are, they have to be linked directly to a framework where local bargaining groups have some sanction.[7]

This means either looking more to the activities of the unions outside the company, or relying on statutory legal rights.

Scandinavia

At the beginning of Chapter 4 we noted the distinction that can be made between the concepts of *zero-sum* bargaining (or if I win then you lose), and *positive-sum* bargaining, where both parties cooperate to produce a mutual gain. Although collective bargaining in the real world is seldom entirely one or the other, many writers have alleged that the bargaining systems of the Scandinavian countries are as close to positive-sum bargaining as we are likely to find.

In Sweden for example, the "Swedish model" of wage bargaining was characterized until recently by central negotiations between the Swedish employers federation (SAF) and the central federation of manual workers union (LO), and between the SAF and the private-sector white-collar union centers, with the object of agreeing to an acceptable level of wage increases for that year. Once this was established, the individual industrial unions would commence negotiations with the employers in their particular industry, taking the central agreement as a guideline. In these central negotiations the major criterion used by both parties was a preservation of the competitiveness of industries in the exporting sector (as Sweden's small population cannot provide a sufficiently large domestic market to support her major industries, economic growth can only occur through successful international competition). Both SAF and LO have therefore agreed in the past that if short-run wage increases are allowed to outstrip the rate of growth of the export sector the long-run consequences will be to everyone's mutual disadvantage.

This identification by Scandinavian trade unions with the wider society has been strengthened by prolonged periods of social democratic government in both Sweden and Norway and the unions' historically close links with the social democratic parties. In addition, the levels of trade-union membership are the highest in the industrial world, running at 70% of the working population in Norway and 80% in Sweden, and the unions are accorded a much higher status and respectability in society than that found in most other industrial societies, so that to be a "good trade unionist" is virtually synonymous with being "a good Swede."[8]

Following from this social and political status, the other major characteristic of the Swedish model is that, in return for their concessions of moderation and social responsibility in wage bargaining, the unions have come to expect the government to promote favorable legislation in such areas as social welfare, workplace rights, health and safety, and codetermination. The unions see such legislative advances as having the advantage of benefiting all workers and not only those in powerful bargaining positions.

Thus the Scandinavian bargaining systems are noted for basic agreement and joint cooperation (stronger in Norway than in Sweden), the fruits of which are redistributed through legislation. In view of this position, it is not surprising that the unions have used this combination of central bargaining and rights conferred through legislation, to influence the introduction of information technology.

In Norway, for example, as early as 1975 the Norwegian employers, NAF, and the Norwegian LO concluded a basic agreement on new technology that has set both the format for all subsequent local technology agreements and the tone for the treatment of technological change throughout Scandinavia; its basic premise is that in the design, introduction, and use of computer systems, the social consequences must be regarded as being of as equal importance as the economic and technical effects. The agreement stipulated that the unions have the right to information on any aspect of change that affects their members and this information must be couched in nonspecialist language, and must be given sufficiently early to be of use. In order to monitor technological change more effectively, the workforce would be allowed to elect an additional workplace representative in the form of a data steward who was to be allowed any necessary time off for technical training. The extent to which the provisions in this basic agreement have been adopted is indicated by the fact that by 1985 there were 600–700 data stewards in a working population of only 1.9 million.[9]

In Sweden, rather than sign a central basic agreement on technology, the unions have relied on their rights under the 1976 Codetermination at Work Act. This made the union the agency for codetermination in the firm (rather than a separate works council on the German model), and set up the framework for union and management to negotiate local codetermination agreements. Under Swedish codetermination, although management are not required to consult the workforce during the preliminary planning stage, they must initiate discussions and negotiations with the union before any final decisions are made on organizational or technical change. The union can request access to company accounts and internal documents on labor-force policy and production changes to assist their case. Again, information must be made accessible in an easily understood form.

However, what distinguishes the Scandinavian approach to new technology from the average British NTA really derives from the legislation in both Norway and Sweden on the quality of the working environment. The Norwegian Work Environment Act of 1977 emphasizes the necessity for any organizational or technical change to result in a "fully satisfactory work environment" within which the work itself should give people a reasonable opportunity to develop in decision-making. It was this legislation and its counterpart in Sweden that provided the legal framework within which local technology agreements were formulated.

The difference in emphasis can be seen in the treatment of health and safety. Under the Norwegian act, the Labour Inspectorate can issue legally binding regulations to ensure a safe and satisfactory working environment, and the regulations dealing with screen-based equipment have been more concerned with overall system design than merely the technical specifications of the hardware. The training requirements laid down by the Inspectorate cover the role that the VDU task plays in the overall organization, alternative work routines if the hardware breaks down, and the need for adequate breaks. If VDU work is routine then only 50% of the operator's time should be spent at the terminal.[10] The Swedish Work Environment Act of 1978 expanded on earlier joint agreements in the private sector and gave joint working-environment committees in the workplace the right to be consulted on any project changes that had health and safety implications.

How has this comprehensive approach to technological change worked in practice? The introduction of new technology has not been without its problems. The unions soon realized that the speed of change outstripped the ability of legislation to adequately provide safeguards and so have tended to place an increased reliance on collective bargaining.[11] The Swedish unions have similarly been critical of the slowness of the National Board of Occupational Health and Safety to keep its regulations up to date with changes in technology, and of its inability to involve effective sanctions against employers who ignore the guidelines.

At the local level, there is evidence that the unions still feel that they are not sufficiently well-informed to exercise all the influence on the rate and direction of change that they would like. There have been two problems with the right to information: first, the timing and amount of information offered by management and second, the ability to put it to good use. We saw above that under the Swedish codetermination arrangements the unions are unlikely to be informed until after the planning stage, and one survey in mechanical engineering firms found that the workforce felt that the information was still not sufficient to enable them to participate effectively in the decision-making process, and that because the workers' representatives were usually divided into a number of joint study groups it was often difficult to formulate a coordinated response. In response to requests to broaden the basis of participation, management was likely to reply that because so much of the latest technology was of imported foreign manufacture, there was little chance for the workforce to influence design or formulate alternatives. The authors of this critical study concluded that "worker and union influence on the process of introduction was slight or non-existent"[12] and a similar conclusion on the effectiveness of Norwegian data stewards has been made by Gustavson.[13]

The problem of putting the information to use is reflected in the fact that when the Norwegian basic technology agreement was renegotiated in 1978 and again in 1982, it was specifically agreed that the unions could bring in outside technical experts to assist them, and similar provision has been made in some Swedish codetermination agreements (the fees of such consultants to be paid by the employer).[14]

These limitations, far from creating an air of resigned fatalism within the trade union movement, have instead resulted in new initiatives. Central agreements of a new type were signed in the early 1980s on the general theme "workplace and enterprise development," which jointly established guiding principles in the general areas of work organization, technology, and economic issues and resources. That central agreement signed between the LO, SAF, and PTK (white-collar) in 1982 draws on the earlier themes of codetermination and the working environment, and states that:

> Developing and improving the efficiency of the firm, together with safe-guarding the employment, are matters of common interest to the company and its employees.[15]

The aim of such an agreement is to influence the way in which the technology is used in working life, through placing an emphasis on using rather than eliminating the skills and expertise of existing employees, and ensuring that new work is composed of a sound job content and opportunities for employees to exert skills and responsibilities.

In this way, the unions also hope to influence researchers and designers of new systems.[15]

The idea of incorporating existing skills has also been behind several interesting joint and union initiated research projects such as DEMOS, the "democratic planning and control in industry project," an action based cooperation between the unions and academic researchers aimed at helping the unions to clarify their goals within the process of technological change and to formulate alternatives. (We will look at a similar example of action research, the "Utopia" project, at the end of this chapter.)

In assessing the overall success of the Scandinavian approach to handling technological change, we are forced to agree that the approach has been accompanied by a minimum of overt conflict and high level of attention paid to those aspects of change often ignored by technology bargaining in other societies—the content of the job, the quality of the working environment, and employee participation. Gill has suggested that this is closely linked to prevailing values in the political environment and that it is those nations with long periods of social democratic government and a continuing social consensus between the government and the labor movement (such as Denmark, Norway, Sweden, and to a lesser extent Western Germany), that have paid most attention to the social and employment effects of new technology.[16]

In considering this argument in the late 1980s, it has to be questioned whether the economic prosperity that originally underpinned this consensus has become a thing of the past, and new technology becomes inextricably bound up in this debate. We noted earlier that the adoption of new technology has been one response to economic stagnation in the Western economies, and this stagnation has already placed severe strains on the Scandinavian positive-sum model outlined above, so that Swedish centralized bargaining has started to fragment in recent years. Because most of the postwar period union gains have been based, as we have seen, on fostering continued economic growth through cooperating with management to ensure labor-market peace, the unions and the Social Democratic party have tended to favor new technology as a route back to economic success. Yet, at the same time, new technology has played a small but important part in the fragmentation of the system through its effect on the traditional contours of the employment structure. For example, in the Swedish engineering industry because of the erosion of existing job boundaries brought about by the spread of computerization to the shop floor, the Metalworkers Union has been losing members to the Clerical Workers, the latter tending to recruit employees in newly created jobs, and this has been a contributory factor in causing the Metalworkers to break away from central negotiations through the LO, and reach their own separate agreement with the engineering employers.[17]

Thus, although we can agree with Gill[18] that the example of Scandinavia demonstrates that there are alternative approaches to handling change than simple laissez-faire, it will be interesting to see whether such alternatives prove strong enough to weather the current economic storms.

Japan: The Ultimate Model of Cooperation?

As Western trade unions and industrial management fence warily over the more sensitive areas of computerization, occasionally crossing swords, occasionally drawing blood, they are constantly made aware that far away across the Pacific is a land where such difficulties seem unknown, and where it would appear that management and union joyfully walk together into the rising technological sun. With an established world reputation in electronics, the largest number of robots in productive use, and an increasing number of nonstaffed manufacturing systems, Japan seems to offer a model of the way forward to peaceful technological change with no union-disputed redundancies, no demarcation issues, and no strikes over pay or grading.

Many observers, and indeed the Japanese themselves, claim that one of the major reasons for this lies in the uniqueness of the widely-publicized Japanese system of industrial relations, whose key features can be identified as: (a) lifetime or continuous employment, (b) a seniority-based wage payment system, and (c) enterprise trade unionism.

The young Japanese leaving school or college endeavors to get taken on by one of the large "household names" in Japanese industry such as Toyota, Hitachi, or Mitsubishi. Once employed, he will be expected (and will expect) to stay with that company for the rest of his working life, and indeed it will pay to do so, as the largest ingredient in the pay packet will be based on length of service with the company. The recruitment of school and college graduates means that rather than hiring workers with specific skills or trades, the company takes on green labor that it can train in-house to do those jobs for which it has need; when demand for these jobs slackens, it will retrain these workers to do something else.

This labor-force policy in the context of lifetime employment means that for the large Japanese corporation the labor market could be said to be internal, rather than external as in the Western economies. This in turn means that any trade union organizing these workers has to base its organization along different lines from its Western counterparts as it would be meaningless for the union to organize around specific trades or skills. Instead, a union representing Toyota employees will only represent Toyota workers as they are unlikely to work anywhere else, and it has to represent *all* Toyota workers regardless of their job, as some of this year's assembly workers could be trained to become next year's electricians (the only difference in pay will be that they will have been with the company for one year more and so will be an extra point up on the incremental scale). So the basis for the Japanese trade union movement has become the enterprise, resulting in the Toyota Workers Union, the Nissan Union Federation, and so on. This inevitably means that the union identifies very strongly with the company and its products—if the company does well, the union members stand to do well.

Even this extremely simplified account of the Japanese system suggests immediately several ways in which technological change may be accommodated with less friction than in Europe and North America. It can be seen that an internal labor market is more flexible in its ability to redirect labor, that workers will not necessarily lose out financially by changing to another job, and that the trade unions will have a vested interest in maintaining the competitiveness of "their" firm.

By themselves, however, these factors would be insufficient to account totally for stress-free change for there are two other factors that must be mentioned. The first is the nature of the Japanese corporation itself, which tends to be a multiproduct organization often straddling very different industries (the Yamaha that makes the motorbike is the same Yamaha that makes the musical instruments). Thus, the Japanese enterprise is often able to cope with downturns in a single product market by transferring workers to another division of the company or a subsidiary whose products are currently faring better (the transfer to a subsidiary being known as "amakiduri" or "descent from heaven"). A survey by one of the national industrial union federations, Denki Roren (the Federation of Electrical Machine Workers Unions), in 1983 found that in 60% of workplaces where microelectronics-based technology had been introduced, the workforce had decreased, but that this had been almost entirely achieved by the transfer of workers to other workplaces.[19] This might entail a considerable geographical distance for the worker and a separation from his family. The degree to which the worker "belongs" to the firm however means that these demands are accepted to a degree unlikely to be found in Western labor movements.

The second and probably major factor behind the absorption of new technology however lies in the fact that the famed "Japanese system" probably applies to only about a third of the total Japanese labor force. For the economy as a whole, as opposed to the individual large corporations, Japan presents an almost pure form of a dual labor market, only one half of which corresponds to the terms and conditions of employment outlined above. The large corporations, in addition to their regular workers, hire large numbers of temporary workers (often seasonal workers from the countryside) and part-timers (often women). Indeed, the role of women lies almost entirely outside the lifetime employment system as after their early 20s they are under strong pressure to leave and get married, returning later in their lives as part-time workers. These temporary and part-time workers are all on short-term renewable contracts and not covered by either lifetime employment or the seniority payment system; indeed, it can be seen that their existence is one of the reasons why the enterprise can offer such terms to its core of regular workers. It can also be seen that such part-timers offer a ready source of natural wastage. As the government-funded Japan External Trade Organization states quite candidly:

> . . . robotization in Japanese companies takes place slowly, step by step. Robots are introduced first to only part of a production line, most often to a section where the labor force is composed mostly of female workers. Since women in Japanese companies typically leave after two or three years to get married, robots can move in smoothly with no lay-offs or dislocations.[20]

We have so far spoken only of the large corporation sector; the other half of the Japanese dual economy is comprised of the myriad of small and medium firms who mainly exist to serve the giants on a subcontracting basis. These smaller firms, though they try to emulate the giants, do not have the resources to offer either the promise of perpetual job security or the company welfare provisions that the big firms can provide, and employment in this sector more closely resembles the external labor markets of the West. As one of the ways in which the large corporations weather downturns in demand is typically to take subcontracting work back in-house, the small firm sector again provides a hidden source of labor flexibility that enables the flagship companies of the Japanese economy to sail on relatively unscathed.

As neither temporary, part-time, female or small-firm workers are usually unionized, we must be a little careful in interpreting the published attitudes of Japanese union leaders to microelectronics change. The enterprise unions represent workers who will not lose their jobs or their seniority-based pay, and who could be retrained to work the new equipment. Thus, it becomes understandable that most accounts of new technology introduction emphasize the degree of joint consultation between management and union prior to introduction and the generally positive attitudes expressed by enterprise union leaders towards new technology in general. Nissan, for example, which has over 1,000 robots in use, could still sign an agreement in 1983 with the Nissan union that promised to advise the union in advance of further robotization, neither to lay off nor downgrade workers replaced by robots, and to provide retraining for those affected.

Undoubtedly the Japanese employment system makes such rapid adjustment possible for the large corporation. However, although in the short term new technology may be intensifying the degree of integration between the enterprise union and corporate management, over a longer period it is creating severe tensions within the Japanese system.[21]

Whereas existing regular employees are maintained on the payroll, as in the above example, the recruitment of school graduates as future regular workers declines or stops altogether as the company relies more and more on temporary workers to meet any sudden increases in demand. Thus, over time, the percentage of regular workers in the labor force is bound to decline, a trend accelerated by the deskilling effects of new technology as it is lesser skilled repetitive jobs that tend to be performed by part-time and temporary workers. Changes in the skills required will also weaken the system of seniority-based payment that contains a built-in assumption of a link between seniority, acquired skills, and merit. The necessity to quickly obtain workers with computer-based skills (which tend to be less accessible to older workers), has forced several firms to place less reliance on seniority and use other cash incentives to attract and hold such employees; indeed, in some areas of the corporation such as research and development where creativity and innovation are important, the seniority principle is disappearing fast.[22]

The decline in the number of regular workers also means a decline in union membership, a trend that is already happening. Unionization in Japan has dropped from 35% in 1970 to 31% by 1981, and the federation of enterprise unions in engineering, Denki Roren, reported a drop of 13% in the membership of its affiliated unions through robotization alone. One union attempted to solve this problem in very Japanese fashion: in 1982, at the Fujitsu Fanuc plant where increasingly robots help to make robots, the plant union became concerned that falling membership, through transfers of staff to other plants, was having a serious effect on union funds. After prolonged consultation, management and union agreed: the robots would become honorary union members and a subscription for every robot would be paid by the company into the union coffers. Unfortunately this arrangement, enthusiastically copied by several other firms, was ruled out of order in the Japanese Labor Court as it was found to constitute company payment to union funds which is illegal under the labor regulations.

So despite its superficial attractiveness to Western management, the Japanese system does not contain any magic ingredients for problem-free change. The present jobs of an elite or "labor-aristocracy" of regular unionized workers are guaranteed, but this is only made possible by the ability of the large firms to transfer workers to other plants or to subsidiary firms, and already there are severe doubts in Japan about the ability of the lifetime employment system to survive. Such guarantees do not apply to all the rest of the labor force.

If Japan does point the way at all to other industrial societies it may be in terms of the future for aggregate patterns of employment. The long-term prospects for Japan examined above would seem to lend support to the prediction we encountered in Chapter 2 of a polarization of the labor market between a small elite of skilled employees, probably retained by their employers through all fluctuations in demand, and the deskilled majority who can increasingly only be expected to work on short-term contracts. We will examine this and similar predictions more fully in Chapter 6.

The Lessons of Cooperation

What can be concluded from this examination of three widely differing examples of nonconflictual approaches to technological change? Although there is some evidence that such approaches have been able more adequately to tackle areas such as job content and quality of work, they seem only to stand a chance of success either if the workers concerned divorce themselves from the interests of the rest of the workforce as in the case of Japan, or if the wider industrial relations system or dominant values in society place an emphasis on the possibility of common interests, as in the case of Scandinavia. Even in the latter instance, this does not prevent conflictual issues from emerging, as evidenced by the strikes in West Germany and the recent breakdown of the centralized Swedish bargaining system. We noted that the European Trade Union Institute report concluded that even where there were substantial legal rights of codetermination at the workplace, some effective bargaining structure was necessary to make this worker participation at all influential.

Where there is no generally accepted social value placed on shared interest however and the actors in the industrial relations system assume that their interests will normally be mutually divergent, then cooperative approaches and experiments face an uphill struggle and are often doomed to failure. In Britain, in 1981, the TUC's attempt to get a joint policy statement on new technology was rejected by the Confederation of British Industry, whereas in Australia, where the unions employers and the government did succeed in issuing a tripartite technology policy, a survey of companies in Victoria showed that virtually no one had heard of it, and those that had were largely ignoring it.[23]

For this reason, recent management-inspired attempts in Britain at "user-involvement" in job redesign schemes have generally been viewed with the suspicion that they are the latest in what the unions see as a long line of "phoney participation" ventures in British industrial relations. This view is however not universal, and it is the area of job redesign that has been hailed by some as the positive way out of the traditional industrial relations impasse.

JOB REDESIGN

In Chapter 4, we noted that the ability of NTAs to minimize overt conflicts of interest and to lay the procedural framework for technological change was limited in two key ways. First, by the current relatively weak position of the trade unions in most industrial societies, which has enabled some employers to resist requests for new technology bargaining altogether or, where bargaining does take place, has ensured that the terms attained often fall far short of the unions' stated "model" agreements. Second, they are limited by the fact that traditional collective bargaining, especially in Britain and the United States, has more often than not been quantitative rather than qualitative, in which unions strive to increase or maintain tangible concrete goals as measured in terms of cash or hours worked. Bargaining over the content or *quality* of work has not been a conspicuous feature of collective bargaining (although developments in health and safety bargaining were a move in this direction). For example, taking action to ensure that a nominally ''skilled'' job remains filled by members of a particular craft union, despite the fact that the contents of the job may have altered over the years and may no longer actually need a long period of craft apprenticeship, is not the same thing as trying to ensure that the job itself is not deskilled.

We noted in Chapter 3 that the way industrial organization has been developed in the pursuit of the goals of competitiveness and profitability has in many cases been characterized by a general deskilling of occupations, as complex tasks were fragmented into single subtasks performable by cheaper labor, and the removal of any mental operations from the job, either incorporating these in the machine or transferring them to the responsibility of specialist planners or production engineers. In examining the predictions of those who see the introduction of new technology as a further step in this process and one that introduces it to hitherto untouched areas such as the office, we saw that although this did not appear to be *technically* inevitable, there was at present strong evidence that this was occurring in a significant number of locations.

The dominant legacy of F.W. Taylor's ''Scientific Management'' in mainstream managerial thought created a long-lasting perceived wisdom that for many years saw such developments as only being good for the enterprise. The major management problem thus became to find adequate means of motivating individual workers to perform these tasks within the required standards.

Later developments in academic and management thought have slightly dented the dominance of this view and led to some modifications. The rediscovery that there might conceivably be some psychological satisfaction to be had from doing certain types of work, and that there were social satisfactions arising in the work place from the social organization of work, led to the movement from the 1950s onward that jobs should be ''re-designed'' to take these additional (yet still motivational) factors into consideration. Formerly separate subtasks were taken and reconstituted in a variety of ways to make a more complex and (it was hoped) interesting whole.

Although such ideas cannot be said ever to have superceded the minute division of labor as the guiding principle of work organization,

they have had a considerable resurgence with the arrival of new technology and the fundamental changes in the organization that accom-
pany it. There are two major features of current attempts at job redesign
around new technology: (a) an increased emphasis on worker participation in the redesign process, and (b) strong support for it from one
or two key unions, who have seen it as a means of overcoming the
deficiencies in new technology bargaining. The British clerical union
APEX points out that although collective agreements focus on the technology and the implications this has for jobs, job redesign starts with
the job content and then works towards the implications for technology
and managerial practice. Thus, its supporters hope, the horse is put
back in front of the cart.

What then is job redesign? APEX has defined it as:

> The organisation of tasks in such a manner as to structure jobs which will
> provide job satisfaction, make full use of the ability of job holders and to
> allow access to facilities which ensure proper career progression.[24]

The overall aim is to ensure that "routine and monotony are mini-
mised." The promotion of such schemes to tackle the introduction of
new technology is currently being linked to revamp theories of worker
participation with the aim of involving the workforce at every stage in
a joint redesign exercise.

There have traditionally been four major ways in which job redesign has been attempted in the past:

Job Enlargement. Putting together previously fragmented tasks to
increase the cycle time and create a more complex job. This is sometimes called horizontal redesign and, as such, does not meet the criterion of career progression outlined in the quote from APEX; indeed,
it may simply consist of several monotonous tasks put together with
no significant increase in satisfaction.

Job Enrichment. Sometimes referred to as vertical redesign because it aims to reconnect decision-making and responsibility with the
execution of the task.

Semi-Autonomous Workgroups. In which a defined group is given
a significant amount of responsibility for internally organizing the work
in hand and allocating the distribution and sequencing of tasks. The
best known example of this is probably the experiment at the Volvo
Kalmar plant in Sweden.

Quality Control Circles. Workgroups are encouraged to meet and
discuss the organization and production problems of their jobs and to
suggest more rewarding and efficient ways of tackling production prob-

lems. Although the idea originated in America in the 1950s, it is widely associated with the practice of Japanese firms, where it fits in with the internal methods of the Japanese corporation, and has been enthusiastically taken up in some European business quarters as part of the "after Japan" movement that we touched on in the previous section.

Such ideas of job redesign are not new, having been advocated and tried since the 1940s, although the results it must be said have seldom lived up to the expectations.[25] Why have they experienced such a resurgence with the advent of new technology? First, the technical characteristics of computer systems makes user involvement a far more viable option: The spread of networked terminals makes direct user access a feature of such information systems. Second, as we have seen, new technology has the characteristic of organizational flexibility; there is no "one best way" to organize people and the new technological systems. Managers have a choice from continued Taylorism on one hand, resulting in systems characterized by hierarchical organization, emphasis on managerial prerogatives, increased division of labor, and the "industrialization of the office." On the other hand, they can equally choose participative redesign where, rather than simply buying the best "expert design" from an external agency, management and workforce can jointly develop a system that is mutually acceptable and offers gains to all concerned.

The office has been identified by many analysts as the area where we can expect the most profound changes as a result of new technology. It is also likely to be the area where much of the experiments in participative redesign are likely to be focused. Because unionization in the office is still weak or only partial, unions may see their involvement in participative design as a means of strengthening their representational importance. Management for its part may see participative redesign as a means of overcoming the widespread failure of computer systems to match or even approach their technically specified performance levels (see Chapter 4). In the face of potential hostility and suspicion the only route to successful implementation may appear to be through enlisting the involvement of those most likely to resist.

The idea of user involvement in system design initially sounds like a promising way of tackling part of the problem of new technology. The idea, however, contains within it a good many snags that can serve to mar its operation in practice.

APEX see one of the major problem areas to be entrenched attitudes on both sides. Managers are still first inclined to see jobs as being determined by the technology that they feel they have to use,

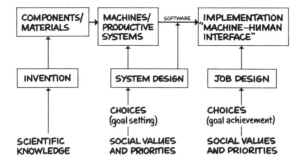

Figure 8. Stages of participation in the development of productive systems.

whereas the workforce may not unnaturally feel that jobs are ultimately about money: a job is but a means to an end ("time sold for money earned"), rather than any source of self-actualization.

Such attitudes are, of course, the product or symptom of decades of industrial development rather than its cause. If technology, following Taylor and Ford, is developed *specifically* to fragment job tasks (as in, for example, assembly-line technology), then that is what it will do; if the jobs created lack any source of fulfillment or autonomous responsibility then they are unlikely to be *expected* to provide these qualities by the workforce.

A major practical problem area concerns the stage at which users are involved in the construction and implementation of computer systems. Ramsay and Beirne identify three major stages in the process: (a) goal-setting, (b) the design of means to achieve the goals, and (c) the implementation and evaluation of the means.[26] The later the users are brought into the process, the more time and money have already been spent and the more inflexible the process is to participative influences. These stages and the possible types of participative intervention are demonstrated in Figure 8. Using this model, we can see that the weakest (or phoniest) form of involvement is that sort of passive user-involvement that takes place at the time of implementation. In this case management, at a fairly senior level, has already chosen a system, the users are then informed and their scope for decision-making amounts to little more than a say in physical layout or an offer to help the suppliers or system designers identify problems in the early period of use (very much an "ironing out the bugs" exercise).

Equally lacking in content is the claim by suppliers or designers to have taken the experience of previous users into account in designing a particular system; so-called "user friendliness." In fact, what they are saying is if the system does not provoke outright hostility, then it is regarded as acceptable. Again there is no attempt to build design around the job, instead design is used to sell the system to the users.

Neither of these token nods toward user involvement really constitutes participative job design. It is the work of the sociotechnical systems writers (based in the British Tavistock Human Relations School) that has seemed most promising in constructing such schemes. The emphasis of writers like Mumford[27] on the equal importance of the social organization of work, as well as its technical organization, leads them to stress the importance of the cooperation of users and designers from the very earliest stages in the development process.

Although some companies and unions have actively promoted joint system design, it is fair to say that the majority on both sides remain fairly skeptical. Where the initiative for participative design has come from management, the unions are likely to suspect that this is not for humanitarian reasons but rather to maximize technical efficiency and to ensure worker acceptance of a set of decisions that management has already made. Where the initiative comes from the union, management in its turn may see it as simply another bargaining ploy by the union to retain as much of the status quo as possible.

Operational problems in job redesign stem mainly from definitions. What is the "system" that is being designed? Is it being built around existing technology such as an installed mainframe? Or, does it consist of operating systems linked to specific hardware such as CAD which is likely to be purchased as a "turnkey" or ready-to-use system (in which the design process takes place outside the company and user-involvement becomes more difficult)? Whatever the hardware, the crucial variable is the software (again increasingly bought off the shelf as a ready-made package). The software mediates between man or woman and machine and largely determines whether the system is conversational, interactive, or simply demands that the user keep it fed with data. Some form of user-involvement in software design would clearly be required in any meaningful redesign of jobs, and it is partly for this reason that technical unions such as the TASS have expressed a wish to extend their membership into the software firms (at present predominantly nonunionized).

Similar problems arise from the practical definition of *users*. To the suppliers of systems, users may simply refer to the buyers, and therefore discussions with senior-management representatives of the company buying their system may be presented as "user-involvement." Even where the system is being developed in-house by the data-processing department staff, their discussion on development may well be with departmental managers rather than the staff who are actually going to use the system. A survey of existing participative-design schemes among firms in Scotland showed that less than 1 in 10 had established a design team that involved the whole user population. Most took the form of management-appointed user representatives, the users only getting involved in the implementation stage where they were asked to help "iron out the bugs"[28]; whereas unions like APEX who supported such schemes were anxious that representation should be through the unions (rather than be used as a means to by-pass the union). They envisaged the formation of a joint union–management steering or working group that jointly agrees on each step and then passes decisions into the normal collective-bargaining machinery for ratification.

Participative design has been attempted in the area of information technology located mainly in the office and there have been significantly fewer attempts to apply it to the area of manufacturing technology. Here it is still the case that research and development into new manufacturing systems is carried out entirely within engineering or purely technical criteria. Rosenbrock, a professor of engineering, has criticized the degree to which those aspects such as ergonomics which impinge on job design are treated very much as an afterthought and are largely determined by technical decisions already made.[29]

Rosenbrock and Cooley have argued that there is no technological necessity why this should be so, or why resulting manufacturing systems should deskill or diminish jobs. They have shown, with prototypes, that it is quite feasible to design "human-centered systems" that actually use and depend on the reserves of skill and experience on the part of the operative. The technology serves to enhance those skills, and the skills thereby enhance the productive process.[30]

Case Study: The Utopia Project

In Scandinavia, they have begun a very interesting and detailed 10-year project that aims to construct alternative technical and organizational systems on the basis of just such a "human centered" participative approach. The Utopia Project represents collaboration between the unions, skilled workers, computer experts, and organizational social scientists. The *utopia* in the title is both a reference to a goal that many have dismissed as "impossible," and also an acronym (in the Scandinavian languages) of "on Training, Technology and Products from the Quality of Work Perspective."

The debate on the quality of working life has been pursued in Scandinavia with greater vigor than in any other industrial societies, and Sweden, very much the forerunner in this debate, has been the locus for considerable research and also some practical experiments in management-initiated job redesign such as the Volvo-Kalmar and Saab-Scania experiments in autonomous work groups.

However by the late 1970s, the trade unions had concluded that it was very difficult to make meaningful changes in the content and organization of work if the productive technology was not altered at the same time. In the case of new microelectronic technology, these difficulties had increased with the tendency of companies to buy systems as ready-made "turn-key" packages. Here the unions' ability to influence the appropriateness of technology at the point of production was virtually limited to saying "yes" or "no" to the package offered by particular suppliers. This was despite the fact that as we have seen countries such as Sweden have a well-developed system of industrial democracy in the workplace. The unions and works councils felt that the degree to which modern productive technology became an obstacle to the realization of their demands for the quality of work was increasing rather than decreasing, as production became increasingly based on scientific or technical expertise locked into the machines rather than the existing skills and experience locked into the workforce.

The Utopia Project's aim is to start from the workforce and draw up technological organizational and training alternatives based on the unions' concern for meaningful jobs, for which the unions would then take sole responsibility for implementation and development at local level. Aware of the limitations, the authors of the initial Project Report point out that it is to demonstrate that "trade union development of technology is a feasible strategy under certain favorable conditions" rather than to produce a model with general applications.[31]

Ultimately, the strategy would be based on cooperation and coordination between individual unions and between the unions and the central project, in which local union priorities would be taken up and turned into technological and organizational solutions at technical development and training institutes run by the unions.

In deciding which areas were most suitable for work, the project members concluded that hardware was inappropriate for trade-union design in view of the high development and investment costs. Software, however, was more promising and was also crucial, as the mediating factor between worker and machine, to the development of increased quality of work. Alternative software "enables a dynamic technology to be created"[32] that can be further developed within each enterprise if suitable alternative training programs are adopted at the same time.

However, those software programs that were linked in a control capacity to specific types of productive hardware (for example, robots or machine tools) again only offered limited scope for change in view of the limits imposed by the assumptions built into the existing design of the machinery. Thus, the project opted instead for involvement in the redesign of those programs dealing with the processing of information, narrowing this down to a choice of two alternatives: (a) systems for text and image processing in the printing and graphics industry, and (b) office automation.

The project opted for the graphics industry option in view of the existing very good links between researchers and the graphics unions, and the fact that the industry had a long experience in dealing with technological change—the first new technology agreement to be signed in Sweden was in the printing industry in 1974. In addition, the unions had a highly developed system of technical stewards who monitored technical change, and the unions and their members possessed a high level of technical awareness and expertise.

The priorities of the project were that any alternative system must reintegrate the present clear division of labor between the planning and execution of the printed product, but at the same time produce an alternative that was a "technical" success, in other words one that worked as efficiently as existing models. In addition, the project team was clear that any alternatives must be based on a process of democratic decision making in any companies concerned, both at the level of production (e.g., over autonomous work groups or control over production planning), and at management level (such as over available budgets and over personnel planning). An immediate problem to be tackled was whether any alternatives should be developed that reduced employment levels, even if this reduction were less than existing technological change created.

A year after the project's inception in 1981 they had identified a choice of two production situations—a daily newspaper, and a graphic workshop for small-scale general printing. The choice was virtually made for them in 1982 when they were approached by the management of a state-owned printing group that was interested in the possibilities of cooperating on the development of an integrated text and image processing system for the electronic make-up of whole newspaper pages.

By 1987, the project reached the prototype stage and in the process came up against some crucial limitations of existing technology when measured against "human-centered" priorities. For example, they concluded that the ideal screen for full-page makeup should have the characteristics of being non-light emitting (that is, be based on liquid crystal or similar technology), have a high resolution, be at least full newspaper-page size, and be flicker-free. The current state of microprocessor and liquid crystal technology cannot produce such a screen: the resolution is too low and the size of screen too small.

Apart from raising the strategic question of whether the unions simply reject all computer systems until the technology is available that will match up to their priorities (which in practice terms they would be unlikely to do), the conclusion to this example from the project seems applicable to do the whole area of interface between machines and people. That is if you start from the standpoint of people's priorities you can quite rapidly reach the limitations of what the technology in its present state has been designed to do; conversely if you start from the basis of the technology, it follows that you are quite likely to be pushing against the limits of human mental and physical well-being.

DISCUSSION QUESTIONS

1. What positive approaches to accommodating technical change in the workplace are suggested by the examples of either West Germany or Sweden?
2. Could the "Japanese model" of adaptation to technology be exported effectively to non-Japanese industrial societies?
3. What conditions should be met by management and workforce to ensure the viability of any participative job-redesign program?

REFERENCES

1. P. Blumberg, *Industrial Democracy: The sociology of participation*, Constable, London (1968).
2. E. Brumlop & U. Juergens, Rationalisation and industrial relations—A case study of Volkswagen, in: O. Jacobi, B. Jessop, H. Kastendieck and M. Regini (eds.) *Technical change, rationalisation, and industrial relations*, Croom Helm, London (1986).

3. I.G. Metall, *Der erste Schritt unserer Gegenwehr* [extracts translated as *The first step in our fight back: First interim report of IGM covenors committee on the rationalization of Opel in Bochum*], Author, Bochum (1984).
4. A. Hingel, A promethean change of industrial relations—A comparative study of Western European unions and technological developments, in: M. Warner (ed.), *Microprocessors, manpower and society,* Gower, Aldershot (1984).
5. G. Bamber & R. Lansbury, Codetermination and technical change in the German automobile industry, *New Technology, Work and Employment, 1* (ii), 1986, pp. 160–171.
6. G. Bamber & R. Lansbury, Codetermination and technical change in the German automobile industry, *New Technology, Work, and Employment, 1* (ii), 1986, pp. 160–171.
7. European Trade Union Institute, *Negotiating technological change,* Author, Brussels (1982), p. 40.
8. S. Lash, The end of neo-corporatism?: The breakdown of centralized bargaining in Sweden'', *British Journal of Industrial Relations, 23*(2), 1985, pp. 215–239.
9. B. Gustavsen, Technology and collective agreements: Some recent Scandinavian developments, *Industrial Relations Journal, 16*(3), 1985, pp. 34–42.
10. European Trade Union Institute, *Negotiating technological change,* Author, Brussels (1982), p. 70.
11. Ruskin College Trade Union Research Unit, *Seminar report: Trade unions, new technology, and the disclosure of company information,* Ruskin College, Oxford (1982), p. 4.
12. J. Ahlin & L. Svensson, New technology in mechanical engineering industry: How can workers gain control?, *Economic and Industrial Democracy, 1*(4), 1980, pp. 487–521.
13. B. Gustavsen, Technology and collective agreements: Some recent Scandinavian developments, *Industrial Relations Journal, 16*(3), 1985, pp. 34–42.
14. European Trade Union Institute, *Negotiating technological change,* Author, Brussels (1982), p. 72.
15. B. Gustavsen, Technology and collective agreements. Some recent Scandinavian developments, *Industrial Relations Journal, 16*(3), 1985, pp. 34–42.
16. C. Gill, *Work, Unemployment and the New Technology,* Polity Press, Cambridge (1985), p. 141.
17. S. Lash, The end of neo-corporatism?: The breakdown of centralized bargaining in Sweden, *British Journal of Industrial Relations, 23* (2), 1985, pp. 215–239.
18. C. Gill, *Work, Unemployment, and the New Technology,* Polity Press, Cambridge (1985), pp. 159–160.
19. R. Whymant, The cradle to the grave system is taking a battering in Japan, *Guardian,* August 17, 1983.
20. Japan External Trade Organization, Industrial robots, *Now in Japan* (No. 32), Author, Tokyo (1981), p. 15.
21. A. Ishikawa, Microelectronics and Japanese industrial relations, in: M. Warner (ed.), *Microprocessors, manpower, and society,* Gower, Aldershot (1984), pp. 349–360.
22. T. Nuki, The effect of microelectronics on the Japanese style of management, *Labour & Society;* Vol. 8(4), 1983, pp. 393–400.
23. Australian Trade Union Handbook, *Technology and union response,* Trade Union Information and Research Centre, Sydney (1984).

24. Association of Professional, Executive, Clerical and Computer Staff, *Job design and new technology,* Author, London (1985), p. 3.
25. H. Ramsay, What is participation for? in: D. Knight, H. Willmott, & D. Collinson (eds.), *Job redesign—Critical perspectives on the labor process,* Gower, Aldershot (1985), pp. 52–80.
26. H. Ramsay & M. Beirne, *Computer redesign and "labor process" theory: Towards a critical appraisal,* Department of Industrial Relations, University of Strathclyde (1986).
27. E. Mumford & D. Henshaw, *Participative approach to computer systems design,* Associated Business Press, London (1979).
28. H. Ramsay & M. Beirne, *Computer redesign and "labor process" theory: Towards a critical reappraisal,* Department of Industrial Relations, University of Strathclyde (1986).
29. H. Rosenbrock, Social and engineering design of an FMS, paper to CAPE 83, Amsterdam (1983).
30. M. Cooley, *The new technology—Social impacts and human centered alternatives,* Technology Policy Group Occasional Paper 4, Open University, Milton Keynes (1983).
31. Utopia Project, *Report No. 2,* Arbetslivcentrum, Stockholm (1981).
32. Utopia Project, *Report No. 2,* Arbetslivcentrum, Stockholm (1981).

6

THEORIES OF THE INFORMATION SOCIETY
WHO GETS PLUGGED IN?

Where is the wisdom we have lost in knowledge?
Where is the knowledge we have lost in information?
T.S. Eliot, *The Rock* (1934)

PROFILE OF AN INFORMATION SOCIETY

We have demonstrated that microelectronics has the potential to alter substantially both the quantity and the quality of work that is offered; but, as has already been cautioned, when we say it can do such a thing, this is merely a linguistic shorthand. We have seen that the way information technology develops, how it is used, and what it is used for, are all the result of essentially social, not technological, processes and relationships.

Included in many of the descriptions and analyses of technological change that we have encountered have been, perhaps not surprisingly, some questioning and even prediction about the likely outcome of such widespread alterations to aspects of our social and economic organization. As has been shown, there are those who see the present changes in our patterns of work and employment as the harbingers of a coming social transformation that will be as historically momentous as that of the first industrial revolution and that will transform our whole society into a new type of society—no longer an industrial but an information society. Daniel Bell (pursuing his theme of "postindustrialism") has hailed the "information society,"[1] Tom Stonier has discerned "the third industrial revolution,"[2] Yoneji Masuda (author of *The Japanese Plan for an Information Society*) predicts a future "Computopia,"[3] while the futurologist Alvin Toffler warns us to be prepared for the "third wave" of historical transformation, from whose effects virtually no one on the planet will be immune.[4]

Although blueprints for the future such as these are always noticeably diverse, an attempt to cull the major features of the information society from the different accounts produces a list similar to the following:

- There will be a shift in the occupational structure marked by a growing predominance in the number of "information workers."
- Despite this trend there will be a smaller stock of jobs that resemble current paid employment.
- However, the ones that do exist will be so productive that we will no longer all need to work, nor to work a 5-day week in order that living standards be maintained and improved.
- Work will be intrinsically more rewarding and performed in more pleasant surroundings compared to the boring and frequently unhealthy jobs that industrialism currently offers its workers.
- The work–home distinction will be broken as remote terminals make the prospect of working at home a reality for many. (In this sense, it will be a "revolution" in the original philosophical sense of a wheel turning full circle).
- The shorter working week, greater productivity of the new technology and the end of the work–home divide mean that the information society will also be a leisure society.
- There will be a necessity fundamentally to change the prevailing work ethic that only accords value and status to paid employment.

- The information society will be characterized by a decline in overt conflict between groups in society.

Despite the high-tech gloss, there is in reality very little that is new in such predictions, as writers have been examining the entrails of industrialism for the past half century, trying to spot signs of a new evolutionary stage of societal development. The reader who sensibly asks why they should want to do this, should understand that it is essentially the continuation of a debate with a somewhat bad-tempered, frequently impecunious German who died a hundred years ago. Marx's critique of the capitalist organization of society was so fundamental that, whether or not subsequent scholars have agreed with his political beliefs, it has formed the basis for all subsequent analysis of industrialism. Much of this analysis has had the implicit aim of either proving that Marx's predictions were wrong or alternatively of showing that while he might have been an astute observer of his own time his analysis is no longer useful due to significant changes that have taken place since.

A slight recapitulation is therefore necessary here on the postwar development of theories about the sort of society that we live in. In the 1950s and 1960s, there was a concerted effort to show that although Marx's analysis of capitalism may have had some relevance in the context of the depression and economic disasters of the 1920s and 1930s, in the new postwar world of full employment, governments now knew (thanks to John Maynard Keynes) how to manage economies. Most of the industrial nations had taken basic infrastructural industries into public ownership and it was proclaimed on the basis of these and other changes that old-style capitalism and its attendant class conflict had been superceded and replaced by an industrial postcapitalism.

By the end of the 1960s, as the manufacturing base began to falter, this model in turn gave way to predictions of a postindustrial society. The significant contemporary social changes were taken to be shifts in the occupational structure (see page 158) which suggested that service-based rather than manufacturing jobs were becoming the most characteristic form of employment: the postindustrial society was to be a service economy. However, no sooner had this postindustrial service economy appeared on the horizon than a new technology also appeared that threatened to rob it of its employment potential. So attention has now turned to speculating about the sort of society that the new information technology might be ushering in.

The information society whose embryonic form is being discerned today can therefore be seen as post-postindustrialism. Although the model is less rooted in political economy than its forebears, sometimes appearing to be not much more than a set of technological predictions, its key features do contain legacies of earlier concerns about the nature of industrialism and its potential successors.

Whereas it is beyond the remit of this book to evaluate some of the wider societal predictions, such as Masuda's prediction of class-lessness or Nora's claim that capitalism and Marxism will both be obsolete, it can be seen that much of the information-society model hinges around changes in the organization of work that we can attempt to assess. It may be that if we find little evidence for some of the more sweeping statements about work and employment, then we might be justified in questioning the predictive value of the rest of the model.

The Changing Occupational Structure

The New Zealand economist A.G.B. Fisher, writing in 1935, is credited for being the first to use the threefold classification of the industrial workforce (later refined by Colin Clark in 1940 and many other writers since) as being made up of:

1. Primary workers engaged in agriculture, lumbering, and extractive processes such as coal mining.
2. Secondary workers (industrial manufacturing) engaged on transforming raw materials into products.
3. Tertiary workers engaged in providing not products but services such as transport, retailing, and banking.

This distinction was intended to be not just a classification but a tool for analyzing the historical path of industrial development. It was argued that just as the historical development of industrialism initially diminished the proportion of the primary sector in relation to the number of secondary workers so, as industrial societies matured and an increase in manufacturing productivity was matched by an increasing demand for such intangibles as health services, education, and recreation, there would be a similar reduction in the size of the secondary sector and a corresponding rise in the proportion of service workers.

There is indeed some evidence that this has happened. By the mid-1950s, less than 50% of the working population was employed in the production of food and commodities in the United States; this occurred in the United Kingdom about a decade later, and for the European economic community as a whole by the 1970s.[5] The existence of such trends should not simply be seen as lending support to some sterile academic argument, but as having significant implications for government economic and industrial policy. In the context of the current decline in industrial employment, it has been argued for some years that it is in the continued growth of personal services such as tourism, and financial and social services, that future new jobs will lie. Consequently, as stated, the fact that information technology makes these very employment areas (banking, insurance, and the administration of public social services) vulnerable to automation for the first time, threatens the potential of a service economy to take up fully the employment of discarded industrial jobs.

It is in this context that a new generation of writers has asserted not that we have to reject the above three-stage developmental model, but rather that we need to amend the classification. The service-sector category was getting too unwieldy and imprecise anyway, including everyone from plumbers and hairdressers to professors of economics. Because the lead technology of the current era is undoubtedly the computer, a device that is essentially a communicator as much as a calculator, then it is argued we now have to add a fourth category:

4. Quaternary or information workers. These are all those that are involved in the transmission, processing and receiving of information.

Information is seen to include words, images, numbers, and forms which represent claims on tangible items (money, checks, bills, tickets, deeds, invoices).[8] Information workers work with typewriters, pens, cameras, television and radio, printing presses, telecommunications, blackboard and chalk, and computers.

The information sector therefore includes banking and insurance, education, all media and communications, all office work, journalism, publishing and printing, entertainment and the arts, architecture, computer software and systems design, and even the church. Attempts to estimate the current size of this new sector of the workforce put it at about 41% of the labor force in the United Kingdom and 46% in the United States,[9] although it is further suggested that we can distinguish, within this obviously very diverse category, between *primary* information workers, or those whose end product is information of some form (e.g., teachers or broadcasters) and *secondary* information work-

PROPORTION OF THE
EMPLOYED POPULATION %

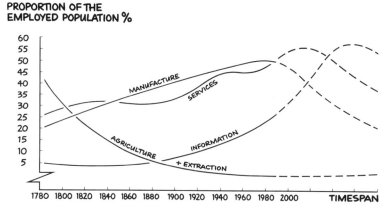

Figure 9. The suggested development model of the "information society." (This is intended as a pictorial representation of the supposed shifts in the occupational structure. It is not an accurate statistical graph of any one society.)

ers who provide information as an input to the production of commodities (such as word processor operators or drawing-office staff).

The projections concerning the growth of the quaternary sector in the information society are based on the prediction that the diffusion and availability of information technology will be so great as to lead to a massive reduction in the cost of information and thus an increase in the demand for information services. This will eventually become the preponderant area of work, leaving the previous three categories as existing in residual form only, just as agriculture has been within the industrial society. A stylized representation of these trends is shown in Figure 9.

Information-society theorists admit that information and services on their own would not sustain an economy. A country like the United Kingdom would need to retain a highly capital-intensive manufacturing base "employing few but precious people,"[10] but the idea that only the manufacturing sector should be viewed as wealth-creating is, they claim, sadly out of date. Tom Stonier asserts that services and information must no longer be viewed as parasitic sectors that exist on the backs of primary and secondary activity.[11] The postindustrial society will therefore be an information society, with information workers not only as the predominant sector of the labor force, but also as the new social class that imprints its stamp upon the political and social priorities of the society.

Despite its initial appeal, there is a lot of ambiguity in this model. One problem with this analysis is that it is not really based on new forms of work but on a reclassification of existing jobs. Most of these "information" occupations already exist within the classification of "industrial" (for example typists, switchboard operators, managers) and "service" workers (such as teachers, advertising, public relations). To some extent, therefore, the above trends are bound to be a self-fulfilling prophecy. If, instead of classifying typists working for a steel company as secondary workers, or teachers as tertiary workers, we reclassify them both as information workers, then the information sector is bound to increase and the others to decrease. But quite clearly nothing has changed except the way we classify our statistics.

Notwithstanding the suggested category of "secondary information worker," to say that the office workers and designers in a manufacturing firm are involved in something totally different from the production workers verges on a sleight of hand and infers that making things can be done without information. Moreover, as we noted in Chapter 3, the major reason you can identify "information workers" within the productive enterprise is because the processes of conception and execution of tasks have been separated through the deliberate development of the functional division of labor.

Finally, the idea that "information" will provide a growth area for employment in the same way that early industry did is based on an over-simplistic understanding of history (which does not repeat itself in such comfortable and convenient ways). Early industry was very labor-intensive, whereas information technology, in contrast, is both labor-saving and capital-saving, and is thus likely to freeze the rate of growth of employment in the information sector as much as in the other sectors of the economy. Thus, although most OECD countries showed a continued rate of growth during the period 1951–1980 in the proportion of the economically active population primarily concerned with handling and storing information, the rate of growth of this sector in the last decade, 1970–1980, has actuallly slowed down at the very time when information technology has been making its debut.[12]

Changing Patterns of Work

The second in our list of key features of any supposed postindustrial society is the decline of full-time regular employment as the arbiter of what is and is not socially defined "work." Initially, the evidence for this seems far more substantial: there is no doubt that in the late 1980s there are significant changes going on in patterns of work and employment. The question is whether these are so qualitatively different from those changes in work organization that have accompanied technical development in the past as to warrant being hailed as signs of a new social order.

We have already noted that modern corporations increasingly compete more in terms of quality and design than market price, and that new technology is seen here as an aid in reducing lead-time from drawing board to product. These changing patterns of production, away from relying on long runs of a standard single product towards a frequently changing product mix have, it is claimed, created a need for flexible production systems and in turn for a more flexible workforce. At the same time, persistent high levels of unemployment in the industrial nations and the ensuing weaknesses of the unions have provided employers with opportunities to bring about the desired changes.

Atkinson has identified three potential areas of workforce flexibility in the contemporary firm: (a) numerical flexibility, in which the firm can more easily alter the size of its workforce to meet fluctuations in prevailing demand; (b) functional flexibility, in which traditional demarcation lines between one craft and another or between craft and noncraft jobs disappear in favor of cross-trade working and multidisciplinary workteams; and (c) financial flexibility involving a shift to new pay and remuneration systems.[13] It is alleged that the modern corporation that takes these as its goals will divide its workforce horizontally between a primary core of full-time multiskilled employees and a larger secondary group of peripheral workers composed of unskilled workers on short-term contracts, part-timers, temporary workers, and outworkers. Other tasks (e.g., maintenance and overhaul work) will be increasingly "outsourced" to subcontractors and agencies.

It is further suggested that the result of these developments will be that the two different sectors of the labor market will be treated very differently by the employer. The secondary or peripheral sector will be subject to the forces of supply and demand to a greater extent than at present (several European countries have recently repealed or modified their legislation to make hiring and firing an easier process for the employer); they will be subject to traditional directive-management styles and paid very much a flat fee for specific services demanded. The smaller core of primary workers, however, are more likely to be seen as a resource by management and be involved in participatory forms of decision-making and subject to performance-based pay. Their long-term employment in the company will feature frequent periods of retraining and changing trades, equipping them with company-specific skills that are not widely transferable in the outside labor market.

The proponents of this model point to the increase in the proportion of part-time workers from 1981–1986 from 21% to 23% of the British employed population, whereas 6% of the 1985 workforce was in temporary work. However, a recent comprehensive survey of the evidence points out that only a small proportion of these part-timers work in manufacturing and also that the numbers of part-timers in manufacturing actually fell over this period.[14] Most part-timers and temporary workers continue to work in the public and private service sectors and the rise in their numbers must be partly due to the continuing shift of employment from manufacturing to services that we mentioned in the previous section. Only 2% of the manufacturing workforce were on temporary and short-term contracts and these were mainly secretarial.

So, although there may be some examples in existence of the horizontally segmented flexible firm, the evidence for the widespread adoption of numerical flexibility as a deliberate personnel policy seems slight. Moves to functional flexibility are a little more substantiated. Firms entering the United Kingdom such as Nissan have signed highly publicized flexibility deals with the union, and in 1987 the two sides in the British engineering industry nearly concluded a wide-ranging flexibility agreement that aimed largely to do away with traditional job boundaries in the industry; (not easy in a multiunion industrial relations system like Britain, where different trades have traditionally been organized by different unions).

Computerized technology runs like a thread through all these developments. As we have seen, it makes flexible production and manufacturing not only desirable but possible, and the electronic–mechanical mix of technology in the modern machine and the grouping of machines with different functions into clusters like machining centers makes the multicraft worker increasingly more important, and blurs distinctions between craft and noncraft jobs; at the same time the numbers of such workers required are likely to be lower than in older production systems. Similarly, we have seen that the use of terminals, keyboards, and VDUs in both office and shopfloor locations begins to make irrelevant traditional distinctions between manual and white-collar work, making harmonization of conditions and the eventual move to single-status working a logical development.

We have also seen that the capital investment tied up in computerized technology (a technology in which individual systems can rapidly become outdated) necessitates a quick return, and that this has prompted management to go for continuous running in both production and office areas. This has come about at the same time as the unions, in their own response to technological change, have demanded shorter working hours but with no reduction in earnings. In Britain, the problems for management of reducing working hours have been compounded by the high levels of systematic overtime (Britain is the only European country with no maximum to the number of hours that can be worked). Although overtime suited management to the extent that it provided a crude form of labor flexibility and also helped to keep basic wage rates low, it had the effect of making reductions in basic hours doubly costly as often the actual hours worked stayed the same but overtime increased.

In the late 1980s, the need for continuous running of plant (and increasingly of office equipment), and the vogue for flexibility are resolving management's dilemma. Companies throughout Europe have used the opportunity of negotiating over reduced hours to introduce flexibility agreements that depart from the fixed-length working days. Whereas the average hours worked in, for example, a 3-week period will be 8 or 7½ per day, in any one day workers may be asked to work as many as 10 hours without being eligible for overtime. In addition, employees in both manufacturing and services have had to contend with the introduction of a variety of complicated shift systems, such as twilight shifts and extra or continental shifts. Some of these work patterns, such as the twilight shift and other developments such as job-sharing, are increasingly dominated by specific groups of part-time workers such as women trying to combine a return to the labor market with childrearing; one half of all womens' jobs in Britain are now estimated to be part-time.

If we widen our horizon away from the supposed flexible manufacturing firm to the workforce as a whole, it seems probable that with the shift to more service sector employment there has been a small but significant decline in the proportion of the workforce working a permanent 8-hour day for a single employer. When we combine these recent developments with the likely effects on levels of employment (which we noted in Chapter 2), we may have to agree with Barry Sherman that "the concepts of a job for life, a skill for life, a full-time job or a permanent job have come under extreme pressure"[15] and to admit that the era in which these are regarded as "normal" may never return. We should also be aware, however, that historically such an era was comparatively short-lived and probably not typical of the history of industrialism and the development of industrial labor markets.

Management and the Organization

We have concentrated on analyzing the effects of technological change on the working lives of employees. Until now, our concern has been with current developments and how managers and unions have coped with them. Management has usually had a controlling interest here, through being the initiator of technical change. However, because we are trying to peer into the future, we have to consider the possibility that much of what we currently consider to be management's function will either be irrelevant or will have to radically change its nature. Indeed middle management may be more vulnerable to technological change than many other groups.

Peitchinis has argued that the automated office will not show much improvement in productivity so long as the automation remains limited to secretarial services, simply because the bulk of office costs (75%) are not secretarial but managerial.[16] After all, managers cost their companies a lot of money; in addition to their salaries there are the overhead expenses and the cost of support services such as individual office accommodation, telephones, and secretarial services. Sherman points out that most middle management does not spend its time making sweeping entrepreneurial decisions but rather in decision-making around a limited and forecastable amount of information.[17] The new management information systems are quite capable of processing similar data and indicating one of a restricted range of possible outputs (with the added advantage of not needing a long lunch break).

Instead of accepting this and perhaps participating in the design of systems that complement their own skills, many managers are not making it easy for themselves. While managers have been keen to automate the work of their subordinates, the literature abounds with instances of managerial resistance when technological change impinges on their own jobs.

One of the most common causes is so-called "keyboard fever" or fear of new technologies and an unwillingness to learn based on the fear of being shown up to be a slow learner. This has led to instances of managers being discovered surreptitiously entering the offices at night to "have a go on the computer" where they can make mistakes without anyone seeing them. In one instance, a plan to put an "executive workstation" (a terminal) on the desk of every manager in a particular public-sector department was abandoned because many of them regarded the humble business of keyboarding as "female" work that they would not be able to do (British males being rarely taught typing skills). After several instances of managers calling in their secretaries to type out a small memo on the manager's own terminal, it was realized that it was taking three times as long to generate every item of information. It is widely reported that managers are waiting for the introduction of voice recognition to by-pass the bottleneck (as they see it) of keyboarding in information, but the technical experts indicate that an effective system is a long way off (and the company may not wait that long!).

Plans to replace the personal secretary with remote word-processing facilities have met with even greater resistance, the secretary being the outward and visible sign that the manager has attained a particular position in the organizational hierarchy (see Chapter 2). In addition, secretaries still do all the extra tasks and functions not in the job description but which arise from the predominantly male–female/boss–secretary relationship—bringing in the coffee, watering the plants, booking luncheon appointments, "protecting" her boss from unwelcome callers, none of which can be performed by a collection of circuit boards.

However, it is extremely likely that, in the light of the sort of changes that we have been examining, this clinging to the form of management rather than its substance may only have a limited future. One of the more concrete predictions about a future information society is that the way we organize our productive work is going to change quite radically. Preoccupations with status and hierarchy are products of the large bureaucratic organization with extended vertical chains of command and subordination. The potential that computerization has to decentralize organizational structures could result in what Handy has called the "dispersed" organization, rather than the "gathered" organization that we have at present.[18] In the words of the Nora Report to the President of France, "The workshop will replace the factory . . . the branch office will replace the conglomerate."[19]

In manufacturing, computer-controlled machining centers are likely to make small-batch production much more viable, and can be set up in small group locations supplying the central organization on a subcontract basis (we noted in Chapter 3 that subcontracting of both productive work and services is already on the increase). Handy has used these trends to predict the reemergence of the self-sufficient work group or "gang" as the most common form of work organization.[20] The main obstacles to such developments in the area of production are the high cost of automated capital equipment and the fact that the finished product and raw materials still have to be physically transported: such restrictions do not apply, however, to clerical managerial and technical work as here both the "raw material" and the end product, information, can be transmitted electronically.

The traditional office is based on paper: office workers exchange information by the exchange of pieces of paper. Hence the need for physical proximity—the shorter the distance between the stages in the information flow, the faster the speed of communication. Thus we have become used to the "office-block", the "headquarters complex" and similar physical manifestations of the need to draw many people together under one roof.

From what we have already noted about the characteristics of information technology, it is clear that the electronic information flow does not work like this; the use of remote terminals, word processors, electronic mail, and videofax breaks the link between speed of communication and physical proximity. This raises a large question mark over our current patterns both of organizing work and of commuting to work, especially if once the staff have traveled into the central location from an ever-widening suburban catchment area, management nevertheless proceeds to communicate with them over the computer and the telephone. Management may well seize upon the principle of "terminals not trains" and relocate groups of staff working on a given office function in smaller premises much nearer their homes, these different functional groups to be connected electronically. Although this is technically attractive, there is some evidence from the United States of managerial resistance to such dispersion of their staff; it is rationalized with statements such as "you can't trust people you can't see," but it is more likely that resistance comes from the fear of a loss to the ego of not having visibly large numbers of people working under you.

Again there is the possibility of some of this work being provided by specialist contractors, as is already increasingly the case with design, marketing, and consulting services. It is suggested that such small information service-providing groups would display a significantly different organizational structure from that currently prevailing in the traditional manufacturing concern, less bureaucratic and more akin to the "organic" structure that Burns and Stalker claimed to be typical or organizations typified by change and innovation.[21]

What then is the future for managers? It is clear that the dispersed organization could spell the end for much conventional management. As Handy points out, the literature of management theory is largely devoted to the business of organizing, motivating, and controlling large numbers of people whose time has been purchased. If the prophets of the reorganization of work are correct, most of these concepts would be irrelevant. For those managers remaining, with many of their functions incorporated into smart business-information packages, with the loss of many of the superficial trappings of status, even the loss of the visible sight of a large number of subordinates (replaced instead by remote groups of workers in branch outstations), and perhaps finding their own work monitored, measured, and evaluated by the new technology, it may be that they will feel that their market and work position is more akin to the staff beneath them than to the senior management above. When the first generation of computerized equipment was installed into companies, banks, and finance houses in the mid-1960s, it was one of the factors that sent middle status and midcareer managers rushing to join the rapidly expanding white-collar and professional trade unions.

Crossing the Home–Work Divide

The next stage of this decentralizing process toward the dispersed organization is to question whether the office is needed at all. The simultaneous development of computers and telecommunications makes it now possible for people to work from their homes or even their cars, and this is increasingly an option open to groups such as sales staff, writers, researchers, programmers, consultants, and financial analysts. It is perhaps not surprising that many of the predictions concerning patterns of work in the information society lay considerable emphasis on the supposed increase in working at home. In many cases, this is seen to be not only a different pattern of work but also a more desirable one in that it is supposed to give the employee more discretion over how he or she allocates time between work and family as well as to provide working opportunities for women with dependent children.

The image portrayed of the life of the home-based information worker often verges on the idyllic, usually centered around the concept of the "electronic cottage." The usual ingredients are a professional creative job (editor, writer, consultant), living in congenial surroundings (country cottage, house by the sea), remote yet in touch with the world, clients and colleagues connected through the variety of electronic devices (cellular phone, terminal and modem), and above all a respectable level of affluence. In this idealized picture, the information worker is no longer tied to the rigid dictates of the division of the day into work or "sold" time and "free" time. Work and home life are reunited, and the individual is free to divide his or her day according to the differing priorities of work, home, family, and leisure.

When coupled with the predictions of shorter working hours, this picture is very reminiscent of another utopia. When Marx and Engels wanted to depict life under the future communist society they described how it would be possible for a man to fish in the morning, hunt in the afternoon, and read Plato in the evening. One may assume that the future high-tech version will have the person doing some information processing in the morning, remote electronic shopping in the afternoon, and watching TV at night.

There is no doubt that from the company's point of view, electronic home or remote working can seem an attractive proposition with the advantages of flexibility, potential savings in overheads, and also a spreading of the demands on the company's mainframe into offpeak time, given that few home workers will feel it necessary to work the rigid 9 to 5 of conventional office workers.

If this is economically advantageous in relation to secretarial work, it is even more so for the work of managerial grades. We have seen that the economic cost of employing managers at the workplace (not just their salaries but overheads, administration, secretarial, and support staff) has certainly made some companies think hard about the decentralized manager. In addition, if the managers or specialists are employed from their homes on a contract-only basis, this cuts out the necessity for the organization to pay for all the unproductive time in the normal employment day which, given the above costs, can constitute considerable savings.

These possibilities have led to a lot of publicity being given to examples of "telecommuting," "teleconferencing," or remote networking. One of the best known examples is the Rank Xerox networking scheme, originally introduced to run down the numbers of senior management and reduce city center office costs. Managers are encouraged to become self-employed freelancers (but given the promise of substantial amounts of contract work from the company) and linked to the company's central offices through on-line computers. Other computer companies such as International Computers Limited use home-based programmers but retain them as company employees.[22]

There is as yet, however, little evidence of this becoming a widespread practice; most managers and professionals working from home do not use any computerized technology to communicate with the company (even when they are computer programmers) but rather the old technologies of mail, telephone, and personal visit. More significant is the fact that, despite all the publicity in management journals, most electronic home workers are not managers. A large survey of home working in Japan (where one would imagine such developments to be most advanced) divided work done at home using information technology into clerical services (typing, documentation input, and word processing), the development of computer software, and the work of sales staff.[23] The largest number of home workers were those engaged in clerical work, with the word processor and personal computer dominant "tools of the trade;" there was very little evidence of managerial home working or "telecommuting." Most workers were working as subcontractors on piecework, less than a third being on a direct employment contrast, and the vast majority were women in their 30s and 40s.

The attractions of such work for women with young children are readily apparent. As Werneke has pointed out, the usual pattern is that if a women leaves work for several years in order to care for her children, when she returns she usually finds herself irretrievably behind in her career development.[24] Working at home allows more flexible arrangements, in theory balancing the demands of the work with the demands of the children.

In the United Kingdom, Ursula Huws found that the majority of computerized homeworkers in her survey were professional women doing skilled jobs such as data processing, and choosing to work from home because of the pressure of bringing up a family.[25] However, wages were significantly lower than those paid to colleagues doing the same work in offices, and there was a low incidence of sick pay, holiday pay, or pension schemes. Most of those surveyed found it in practice extremely difficult to draw a line between work and home and found the double demands on their time fairly stressful. Despite working at home for the sake of the children, the presence of small children was the most frequently stated obstacle to good work performance. One respondent commented that when she worked in an office this had been treated as a legitimate job whereas working at home was seen as a hobby, all right as long as it did not interfere with anything else. The most frequent complaint, however, is of isolation, mentioned by two-thirds of respondents in Huws's survey. People do not work only for money. Among the other things that can make work worthwhile, we have to include sociability and the presence of the workgroup. A United States computer systems multinational that has an extensive system of telecommuting for its staff has claimed that the staff have discovered the answer to the problem of social isolation to be the electronic gossip network: jokes, games, conversation pieces, and personal messages can be put in store by anyone and called up by any home-based employee any time he or she chooses to have a work break.[26] Apart from the health and safety considerations, which might suggest that any break should be spent away from the screen, electronic socializing will only work if the individual is part of a large interlocking network. For the freelance, self-employed homeworker this may not be possible, and in any case there is evidence that people do not find that electronic communication is anything like an adequate substitute for face-to-face socializing. Some firms, such as Digital, who introduced teleconferencing for their managers found that the amount of personal travel and meetings actually went up rather than declined, mainly because it was felt that personal reactions were difficult to judge electronically.[27]

We must conclude that presently the high publicity given to a few examples of remote working for (predominantly male) managerial grades has obscured the very different reality faced by the majority of (female) homeworkers. Working at home with new technology is a classic example of a form of work organization that is technically feasible but can be socially stressful. Huws concludes that, although most of the women said they were glad to be home working, it was probably because the options for working mothers are still not very attractive because of lack of child-care facilities and deteriorating public-transport services.

One alternative, as suggested by one or two writers aware of the potential stresses posed by isolated homeworking, might consist of small-group flexitime working for either individual workers or small temporary-work companies in remote work locations, "office shops," or neighborhood clerical centers.[28,29] These would be wired up for electronic working, outside of city centers and closer to home (with perhaps integral child-care facilities). There are presently few signs of such a development.

Working at home is of course not a new phenomenon that has only been brought about by new technology, but has been widely practiced for many years in certain industries such as garment manufacture, hosiery, and children's toys. Over this time, home working has been notorious for the low standards of pay, conditions, and job security as compared to full-time employment at the workplace, reflecting the fact that home workers are invariably non-unionized, isolated, with low-bargaining power, and in an impossible position to take any sort of collective action. As Gill has pointed out, all information technology has done is to widen the range of jobs that can now be performed at home, not only because of the greater accessibility of the technology such as word processors and computers, but also because of the facility that computers have for monitoring output and work performance, thus enabling the "workplace" to be fragmented into the home with no corresponding loss of managerial control.[30]

The Future for Industrial Relations

If only some of these predictions come to pass and there is more home-working, less full-time employment for everyone and equal status for employed and unemployed alike, it must be asked whether "industrial relations" and its current panoply of collective bargaining, trade unions, employers' associations, and industrial action are destined to become obsolete and wither away. We have referred earlier to some of the innovations in human resource policies that have emerged in the 1980s and that reflect the changes in the economic climate and the labor market: flexible working, increased use of part-time workers and subcontracting, non-union policies, and so on. Because of these innovations, there have already been moves to alter the terminology and to replace the term "industrial relations" with such euphemisms as "employee relations" or "human-resource management." Implicit in such trends is the underlying belief that such changes in work organization combined with the current waning bargaining power of the trade unions spell the end of old-style industrial relations, seeming to lend support to the inference of the postindustrial theorists that unions are a form of social organization specific to industrialism and are thus destined to become historical curiosities.

While it must be said that one or two unions act like historical curiosities, the assertion that the new information society will not need institutions such as trade unions seems a little premature. In this chapter, we have seen that pay and conditions for home-workers are generally inferior to those secured for employees working under traditional employment contracts. Not all home-workers will be self-employed and even those working on a subcontract basis may eventually feel the necessity to negotiate more favorable contract prices. The unions already have their suspicions about home and remote working: That without adequate representation home workers may become the twentieth-century equivalent of the exploited outworkers of early industrialism, with the computer terminal replacing the stocking frame or handloom. The difficulties of negotiation and organization here are exactly the same—the problems of isolation and geographic dispersal.

Handy, reviewing the likely working conditions of these groups is one of the few authors to ask, Who will protect them?[31] He suggests that the self-employed could have agents as actors and musicians do (although he fails to mention that these groups also have powerful trade unions), other groups might find a strength in co-ops and professional associations, whereas the unions may return to something more akin to the preindustrial trade guilds—fixing prices and standards for self-employed "journeyman" information workers.

Although there may well be an objective need for trade unions or organizations similar to them, they will only fulfill this role if workers see them as being relevant to the new work situations, and if this is to happen the unions are going to have to be equally as prepared as management to shake up their ideas. Presently, the trade unions continue to be overwhelmingly male-dominated organizations whose very existence and power depends on their members being in (predominantly full-time) employment. Sherman (himself a former union research officer) accuses the unions of seeing the new jobs in the secondary labor market as aberrations and somehow not real, partly because they are mainly for women. If they are not to suffer a loss of influence both at the bargaining and national level, then they will have to represent these new groups of part-time, contract, and even self-employed workers and those workers who are not working–the long-term unemployed– "rather than the working classes as they were before unemployment and technology intervened."[32]

Can we make any other predictions for industrial-relations trends in the near future? Among those that seem the most likely is a continuation of union mergers as a response to the blurring of occupational boundaries due to technological change. In Chapter 4, we saw how the changes in printing technology have forced the British craft print union, the NGA, to pursue merger talks with both the union for nonskilled print workers, SOGAT, and also with the National Union of Journalists. Despite the fact that past relations between all three have at times been fairly strained and that exploratory merger talks have several times broken down, the pressure to create one union for the printing industry is seen as the only logical response to technological change affecting everyone in the industry. Elsewhere, ASTMS and TASS, the two white-collar unions in Britain recruiting technical and professional staff, and whose members are among the first to make large-scale use of information technology, decided to merge to create one union for all technical white-collar staff in manufacturing; once this becomes established it is likely that other clerical and banking unions will be forced to consider joining also.

The direction for mergers may well be affected by another development that seems almost inevitable, the rapid abolition of the old status differences between shopfloor (blue-collar) workers and white-collar staff, where the first group is hourly-paid, works longer hours, and often qualifies for lesser holiday and pension rights than the latter group that is paid monthly, works shorter hours, and is usually spared the indignity of "clocking-on and off." "Harmonization" of terms and conditions, which in practice usually means placing all employees on "staff" status, has gone much further in Scandinavia than the United Kingdom, but we have seen how the use of the same technology on the shop floor and in the office makes harmonization a logical development.

In the earlier models of postindustrialism, there was an assumption that levels of industrial conflict would diminish with the passing of the industrial mode of production, and something of this expectation has passed into some conceptions of the information society. However, whereas it may be true that the older infrastructural "smokestack" industries such as coal, steel, and shipbuilding are declining, the above prediction is based on the assumption that there was something peculiar or unique in these occupations or industries that made them conflict-prone. This is an elementary but common misunderstanding of the nature and the causes of strike action and one which fails to realize that the groups in the working population with both the cause and the ability to contest the terms and conditions of their employment will change with changes in the structure and contours of the economy. Some groups will drop from the militant league table (as happened, for example, in the case of textile workers in the early twentieth century), and other groups will emerge (such as auto workers in the mid-twentieth century). There is presently little reason to suppose that some groups of "information workers" will not find themselves in a similar position in the future. A contemporary illustration is perhaps given by the strike in early 1987 of British telecommunication engineers (not hitherto noted for their strike proneness). Aspects of the strike illustrated that the fact that the telecommunications network is becoming absolutely crucial to the development of computerized information networks had not been lost on the engineers, and had created two relevant attitudes: (a) the feeling that the high value of their work could be better renumerated, and (b) the awareness that their bargaining position has been considerably enhanced. As one strike leader was reported to have declared at a strike meeting in London (referring to recent scandals in the newly-computerized Stock Exchange), "There'll be no insider-dealing once the screens go blank!"

The Meaning of Work and Leisure

We saw in Chapter 2 that most economists are doubtful that the new technology will result in any significant expansion of aggregate employment opportunities. Proponents of the idea of the information society have asserted that such limitation or decline in the amount of paid employment, rather than being socially disastrous, should actually be seen as a sign of social transition. The huge increases in productivity that microelectronics will bring about will mean that we will no longer need to work for so many of our waking hours as we currently do, leaving more time for leisure. Thus, it is argued, the quality of life in the information society will be a significant improvement on the present.

This suggestion needs to be examined critically, because before "less work" can become translated into "more leisure," several conditions have to be met. First, it is clear that for such developments to warrant the appellation "leisure society," they must apply to all or the vast majority of the population available for work, and not just to a lucky minority. It seems unlikely that we could rely on the untrammeled workings of the labor market to bring this about, because the labor market already distributes existing employment opportunities unequally throughout society so that some workers continue to work regular overtime whereas others are denied any job at all.

Second, given that we have already noted that technical change occurs at different rates, it is possible that some industries may never experience the benefits of computerized technology and its advances in productivity. For such sectors, any moves toward reducing individual working time are going to seem prohibitively costly, as we saw in Chapter 4 when noting the stiff opposition to the unions' attempts to shorten the working week in order to spread job opportunities.

If a shorter week for all is seen as politically and socially desirable but the market is unlikely to bring this about, even with the growth of job sharing and part-time working, it may be necessary for the future government to enact some redistributive measures to ensure equal distribution of both the opportunities for work and the rewards from working—perhaps a tax or cross-subsidy from the high-technology to the low-technology sector. Such measures would seem on the face of it politically dubious, and could be criticized on the grounds that they would remove any incentive for the low-technology sector to be innovative.

If these problems seem to represent insuperable obstacles to sharing work, it could be argued that they do not go far enough in their analysis because they take concepts which apply to an industrial society—"work," "labor market," subsidy—and try to apply them to a qualitatively different postindustrial society. Writers such as Barry Jones, Barry Sherman, and Charles Handy have argued that the solution to the problem of work in an information society is not to attempt to distribute small parcels of employment to everyone but to redefine the whole concept of "work" and give rewards and status for all tasks performed both in and out of the employment relationship.

The second precondition for a leisure society is that, if there is going to be less work for all, it must not be at the cost of any reduction in income or status. The basis for this assertion becomes clearer if we pause for a moment to define more precisely what is currently meant by the concepts *work* and *leisure*.

Work, in the sense that is used in such phrases as "going to work," or "work experience," is a strange concept in that it is not based on the content of the task in hand: one person can spend every minute of his or her spare time lovingly dismantling and rebuilding a car engine, which is not labeled work but a hobby (as leisure, in fact). Another can perform the same tasks for a commercial garage and this is labeled work. What has changed is clearly not the task but the context within which it is performed. Work is only "work" when it is performed within the employment relationship, when it is a "job" for which the performer gets a payment in return for selling his or her labor power.

From this definition it follows that not all nonwork time is given over to leisure. Whole groups of the population spend much of their time engaged in physically demanding tasks such as domestic labor which are not classified as work (although they would be if, for example, housewives were employed as cooks, cleaners, garment manufacturers, or child-care staff), but clearly are not leisure. The unemployed have an unlimited amount of nonwork time, yet little of it could justifiably be called leisure. If leisure is seen as the opposite of work, it is not in terms of the way we divide our time but the nature of the economic activity that we fill that time with: leisure, in reality, invariably means consumption. In our leisure activities we consume the products of others' worktime: food, clothing, drink, tobacco, entertainment services such as films, television, and football matches, gas, and sports equipment. Without access to an adequate income, our ability to participate in any of these areas becomes impossible or severely curtailed.

So any transition to a society in which we are all employed less (and perhaps some of us never employed at all) but in which we do not experience any diminution in the quality of our economic and social life would require a new definition of what is seen as valuable work. Not just employment but housework, voluntary work for charities, or domestic maintenance. For these to count as equal, they would have to be rewarded and be given the same status as employment.

Following Handy, we can break down the work that people currently do outside employment into the following: (a) Those market transactions that simply do not get registered in the national accounting. This includes "black" economy of "moonlighting", "homers," and other economic activity that avoids tax and social security records, and also what he calls the "mauve" economy of small self-employed services that are too small to register. (b) The "gray" economy of unpaid work, some of it involuntary such as housework, some voluntary such as do-it-yourself house maintenance, charity work, meals-on-wheels, and so on. All these tasks—cooking, gardening, cleaning, child-care—contribute to the general welfare and we could pay someone to do them for us, in which case they would count as "work": do them ourselves and they are currently nonwork.

So, rather than designate all future nonemployed time as "leisure" and vaguely hope that people will have the money to pay for it, it is suggested that we recognize the fact that people very often want to be useful and accord all forms of work the same status in society. Several immediate problems present themselves, not least that of how the workers, both in and out of employment, will be paid. Among the various suggestions currently being floated are included a basic national wage or "citizens' wage", a negative income tax in which those earning about a defined level of income would pay tax and those below it receive a payment to bring them up to that level, and some sort of national dividend. It must be said however that discussion of these ideas remains restricted to academic circles.

One reason for the probable reluctance of any major political party to even float such ideas is the heavy bundle of cultural attitudes attaching to the value of employment in our society—the so-called "work ethic." The concept, developed parallel with industrialism, that work (employment) is not only economically but morally beneficial to us; that it is the activity of the virtuous. The classic German sociologist Max Weber, studying the origins of early industrial capitalism, noted the way in which the life and conduct of the devout Calvinist with its emphasis on working hard but going without immediate material rewards, dovetailed neatly with the activities of the successful capitalist entrepreneur. Although this "Protestant work ethic" may indeed have contributed to early capital formation in Northern Europe and North America, in subsequent years the emphasis was on the necessity of getting the new emergent working classes to enter the factory and the mill on a regular basis; the work ethic swiftly became inverted from the original idea that it was the Christian's duty to work hard in this life, and came instead to infer that not to be in work made the individual morally inferior and, in the eyes of the dominant culture, to be idle, feckless, and work-shy. It thus became an ideology promoted by those with a vested interest in securing a constant supply of labor through the factory gate and the office door.[34] Rose concludes that it was never fully shared by the workers themselves, most of whom have regularly displayed the "instrumental" attitude to work that you have to work in order to live.[35]

Nevertheless, dominant ideologies are powerful things; they become so much a part of the cultural brickwork of the society that work in the sense of paid employment is still our foremost source of social status. The question, What do you do? when followed by the answer, teacher, plumber, typist, welder, lawyer, etc. is one of our most common mechanisms for pigeon-holing those we meet into a variety of complex status hierarchies. However, as different as the status of the above occupations might be, they are arguably all superior to those groups who are not employed at all. Often the answer to, What do you do? is likely to be qualified by an admission of nonstatus: "I'm *only* a housewife" or "*just* a student," "*just* an old-aged pensioner" or (perhaps worst of all) "I'm afraid I'm unemployed."

This ideology of work even obstructs the way we view leisure. Sherman points out that we tend to feel that leisure, like money, has to be earned by working, which is another reason why the unemployed are unable to feel that they enjoy a life of leisure. In the words of an unemployed teenager from Newcastle, "For the unemployed, leisure is a waste of time."[36] It follows, according to Sherman, that present exhortations that we must develop a "leisure ethic" to match declining employment opportunities are mainly futile as a work ethic and a leisure ethic are mutually incompatible. Those in work can look at those enjoying leisure and ask, Why am I here? and those not in work can look at those working and ask the same question.

So if we are told that industrialism is on the wane and that the future is characterized by more leisure, it must be that this powerful ideology has outlived its historical usefulness. Perhaps society will need a new set of social values that attribute a more accurate assessment of the contribution to social life made by employees and nonemployees, and perhaps these values will be translated into the elimination of the substantial differences in status and rewards which these groups now experience.

INFORMATION, TECHNOLOGY, AND SOCIETY

Finally, we should perhaps draw back a little and ask the questions Technology for what, or Information for what? Many of the descriptions about the future society, "where information is all," make no attempt to assess the quality of this information or what it is used for. The implication seems often to be that more information (and the technology to go with it) spells better times. Yet there are clear dilemmas here, best demonstrated by the phenomenon of the home computer.

By the early 1980s, computers were so small and so cheap that for the first time they became a consumer durable to rank with the TV and the microwave. Many thousands of households in the United States and Europe purchased them, something that would have been undreamed of even a decade earlier. Yet what did the vast majority of the owners of these small, very clever electronic brains use them for?

To play games on! Zapping the Asteroid Mutants or escaping from the Tower of Death both count as information-based activities but can we say that they represent a qualitative improvement in our life-style? I am not saying that in precomputer households everyone spent the time sitting by the fireside reading Shakespeare's sonnets, but perhaps there is an indication here of a point where we should ask what all this is about. For, on a more somber note, while information technology has produced technical marvels for a few, it has not yet touched the many. You or I can get money by pushing a piece of plastic into a hole in the wall, yet thousands of the world's population have to walk several miles a day to get a can of brackish water. Currency dealers half a globe from each other can buy and sell dollars and deutschmarks, sterling, and yen in real time of fractions of a minute, yet all our technology is apparently incapable of preventing old people from dying of cold each winter.

We have seen that the same uncertainties exist over whether more information and more information technology will improve the quality of our working life. It could augment our skills, remove drudgery and prevent further unnecessary depletion of the earth's diminishing resources, or it could isolate us in our homes to process meaningless parcels of information whose part in the commercial process we can only guess at.

These uncertainties make an adequate summary of this chapter, and indeed of this book, a difficult task. We have seen that the widespread application of information technology will bring some new jobs but will spell the end of many others; that it may require the acquisition of new skills but that the way it is likely to be used may remove or diminish existing skills. It can be used to remove the necessity for people to do physically dangerous jobs, but it can bring new hazards of its own. It may be associated with new patterns of working and new ways of negotiating the conditions of work, but as yet such departures are far from widespread. It may increase the amount of our nonwork time but not necessarily the amount of leisure.

The fact that all these observations and many more throughout the book take the form of either/or statements should not be surprising. As we have concluded several times, the technology itself cannot bring about any of these results; it is an agent that enables change to take place but it does not determine how, when, or in what direction. All these remain human decisions made as we have seen on the basis of a complex cluster of social, cultural, economic, and political priorities. As the Nora Report succinctly puts it: "Telematics can facilitate the coming of a new society, but it cannot construct it on its own initiative."[37]

It is the sense of this that is sadly deficient in most of the predictions concerning the information society and the "revolutionary" potential of information technology. There is still the underlying belief that social change and social relationships are determined by technology and that because certain developments are technically possible then they will happen.

At best, this is a form of mysticism which holds that some cosmic force will benevolently guide the path of technological development along the route of social progress. At worst, it is a profoundly undemocratic view that claims "there is no alternative" and that treats the protests of those whose lives are being affected by technical change with admonitions that they "can't stand in the way of technical progress." It could be pointed out that the logical conclusion of this form of reasoning is to say "we have the technical ability to eliminate all life on earth, therefore we should go ahead and do it."

In order to assess just how revolutionary the implications of information technology are, we have to return (yet again) to the first industrial revolution and to repeat several historical observations. First, the industrial revolution did not commence with the invention of the steam engine or indeed any other technological innovation; many of the processes of production remained the same for half a century. What changed however were the social relationships. The true invention of industrialism was not steam but a propertyless workforce forced to sell its labor power on the open market. Second, the industrial revolution was not a particularly benign affair but a period characterized by massive social upheaval, widespread squalor, and appalling working conditions (as well as the suspension of many civil liberties).

These observations do not augur well for the image of information technology as the solution to the current conflicts and problems of industrial employment. If the information technology is an indication of a similar revolutionary shift in the basis of our social and economic relationships, then we should expect the transition to the new type of society to be fraught with the same social upheavals. If it is not revolutionary but simply another stage of technological development in the long history of the industrial/service society, then we should expect working with the new technology to bring about the same mix of satisfactions and boredom, interest and meaninglessness that working with older technological systems has produced since the era of the spinning jenny.

DISCUSSION QUESTIONS

1. Is widespread home or remote working likely? What conditions would be necessary to ensure that home-working provided sources of job satisfaction?
2. In what ways will trade unions and employers' associations have to adapt to changing work patterns associated with the spread of information technology?
3. In an information society, what groups would possess economic and political power?

REFERENCES

1. D. Bell, The social framework of the information society, in: T. Forester (ed.) *The microelectronics revolution,* Blackwell, Oxford (1980), pp. 500–549.
2. T. Stonier, The third industrial revolution—Microprocessors and robots, in: T. Stonier, *Effects of modern technology on workers,* International Metalworkers Federation, Vienna (1979).
3. Y. Masuda, Computopia, in: T. Forester, (ed.) *The information technology revolution,* Blackwell, Oxford (1985), pp. 620–634.
4. A. Toffler, *The third wave,* Bantam, London (1981).
5. K. Kumar, *Prophecy and progress,* Penguin, Harmondsworth (1978), p. 201.
6. T. Stonier, *The wealth of information: A profile of the post-industrial society,* Methuen, London (1982).
7. B. Jones, *Sleepers wake! Technology and the future of work,* Wheatsheaf, Brighton (1982).
8. B. Jones, *Sleepers wake! Technology and the future of work,* Wheatsheaf, Brighton (1982), p. 48.
9. Organization for Economic Cooperation and Development, *Trends in the information economy, Committee for information, computer and communications policy, paper 11,* Author, Paris (1986).
10. C. Handy, *The future of work,* Blackwell, Oxford (1984), p. 35.
11. T. Stonier, *The third industrial revolution,* in: T. Stonier, *Effects of modern technology on workers,* International Metalworkers Federation, Vienna (1979).
12. Organization for Economic Cooperation and Development, *Trends in the information economy,* Committee for information, computer and communications policy, paper 11, Author, Paris (1986).
13. J. Atkinson, *The changing corporation,* in: D. Clutterbuck (ed.) *New Patterns of work,* Gower, Aldershot (1985), pp. 13–34.
14. J. MacInnes, *The question of flexibility,* University of Glasgow Department of Social and Economic Research, Research Paper 5, University of Glasgow (1987).
15. B. Sherman, *Working at leisure,* Methuen, London (1986), p. 120.
16. S. Peitchinis, *Computer technology and employment,* Macmillan, London (1983), p. 52.
17. B. Sherman, *Working at leisure,* Methuen, London (1986), p. 56.

18. C. Handy, *The future of work,* Blackwell, Oxford (1984), pp. 74–75.
19. S. Nora & A. Minc, *The computerization of society,* MIT Press, London (1980), p. 126.
20. C. Handy, *The future of work,* Blackwell, Oxford (1984), pp. 72–73.
21. T. Burns & G. Stalker, *The management of innovation,* Tavistock, London (1961).
22. C. Hakim, *Employers' use of outwork,* Department of Employment Research Paper 4, Her Majesty's Stationery Office, London (1985).
23. M. Nitta, Current state of the home duty work system in Japan, *Japan Labor Bulletin,* Vol. 25(2) 1986, pp. 6–8.
24. D. Werneke, *Microelectronics and office jobs,* International Labor Office, Geneva (1983), p. 66.
25. U. Huws, The new home workers, *New Society,* Vol. 67, No. 1113, 1984, pp. 454–455.
26. Control Data Corporation, Telecommuting, in: D. Clutterbuck (ed.) *New patterns of work,* Gower, Aldershot (1985).
27. B. Sherman, *Working at Leisure,* Methuen, London (1986).
28. D. Werneke, *Microelectronics and office jobs,* International Labor Office, Geneva (1983), p. 67.
29. B. Sherman, *Working at leisure,* Methuen, London (1986), pp. 136–137.
30. C. Gill, *Work, unemployment, and the new technology,* Polity, Cambridge (1985), p. 25.
31. C. Handy, *The future of work,* Blackwell, Oxford (1984), p. 126.
32. B. Sherman, *Working at leisure,* Methuen, London (1986), pp. 148–149.
33. C. Handy, *The future of work,* Blackwell, Oxford (1984), pp. 44–48.
34. P. Anthony, *The ideology of work,* Tavistock, London (1977).
35. M. Rose, *Reworking the work ethic,* Batsford, London (1985).
36. B. Sherman, *Working at leisure,* Methuen, London (1986), p. 189.
37. S. Nora & A. Minc, *The computerization of society,* MIT Press, London (1980), p. 6.

BIBLIOGRAPHY

Advisory Council for Applied Research and Development, *Technological change: Trends and opportunities for the United Kingdom,* Her Majesty's Stationery Office, London (1979).

Ahlin, J. & L. Svensson, New technology in mechanical engineering industry: How can workers gain control?, *Economic and Industrial Democracy, 1*(4), 1980, pp. 487–521.

Anthony, P., *The ideology of work,* Tavistock, London (1977).

Ash, N., Bargaining and technological change, *WEA Studies for Trade Unionists,* Vol. 10(37), Workers Educational Association, London, 1984.

Association of Professional, Executive, Clerical & Computer Staff, *Office technology: The trade union response,* Author, London (1979).

Association of Professional, Executive, Clerical & Computer Staff, *Automation and the office worker,* Author, London (1980).

Association of Professional, Executive, Clerical, & Computer Staff, *New technology, a health and safety report,* Author, London (1985).

Association of Professional, Executive, Clerical, & Computer Staff, *Job design and new technology,* Author, London (1985).

Atkinson, J., The changing corporation, in: D. Clutterbuck (ed.), *New Patterns of Work,* Gower, Aldershot (1985), pp. 13–34.

Australian Trade Union Handbook, *Technology and union response,* Trade Union Information & Research Center, Sydney (June 1984).

Baldry, C., & A. Connolly, Drawing the line: Computer-aided design and the organization of the drawing office, *New Technology, Work, & Employment, 1*(i), (1986), pp. 59–66.

Bamber, G., & R. Lansbury, Codetermination and technical change in the German automobile industry, *New Technology, Work, & Employment, 1*(i), (1986), pp. 160–171.

Banking, Insurance, and Finance Union, *New technology in banking, insurance and finance,* Author, London (1982).

Barron, I., & R. Curnow, *The future with microelectronics,* Open University Press, Milton Keynes (1979).

Bell, D., The social framework of the information society, in: T. Forester (ed.), *The microelectronics revolution,* Blackwell, Oxford, (1980), pp. 500–549.

Bird, E., *Information technology in the office: The impact on womens' jobs,* Equal Opportunities Commission, Manchester (1980).

Blauner, R., *Alienation and freedom,* University of Chicago Press, Chicago (1966).

Blumberg, P., *Industrial democracy: The sociology of participation,* Constable, London (1968).

Bosworth, D. L., (ed.), *The employment consequences of technological change,* Macmillan, London (1983).

Bourner, T., H. Davies, V. Lintner, A. Woods, & M. Woods, The diffusion of microelectronics technology in Southeast England, in: D. Bosworth (ed.), *The employment consequences of technological change,* Macmillan, London (1983).

Braun, E., & P. Senker, *New technology and employment,* Manpower Services Commission, London (July 1982).

Braverman, H., *Labor and monopoly capital: The degradation of labor in the 20th century,* Monthly Review Press, New York (1974).

Brumlop, E., & U. Juergens, Rationalization and industrial relations—A case study of Volkswagen, in: O. Jacobi, B. Jessup, H. Kastendiek, & F. M. Regini (eds.), *Technical change, rationalization and industrial relations,* Croom Helm, London (1986).

Buchanan, D., *Canned cycles & dancing tools: Who's really in control of computer-aided machining?,* Paper to ASTON/UMIST conference on organization and control of the labor process, Manchester (April 1985).

Burns, T., & G. Stalker, *The management of innovation,* Tavistock, London (1961).

Canadian Union of Postal Workers, *Reduced Working Time Now,* Author, Ottawa (1984).

Central Policy Review Staff, *Social and employment implications of microelectronics,* Her Majesty's Stationery Office, London (1978).

Child, J., Managerial strategies, new technology and the labor process, in: D. Knights, H. Willmott, & D. Collinson (eds.), *Job redesign: Critical perspectives on the labor process,* Gower, Aldershot (1985).

Child, J., & M. Tarbuck, The introduction of new technologies: Managerial initiative and union response in British banks, *Industrial Relations Journal, 16*(3), 1985, pp. 19–33.

Clutterbuck, D., (ed.), *New patterns of work,* Gower, Aldershot (1985).

Conference of Socialist Economists, *Microelectronics: Capitalist technology and the working class,* CSE Books, London (1980).

Control Data Corporation, *Telecommuting,* in: D. Clutterbuck (ed.), *New Patterns of Work,* Gower, Aldershot (1985).

Cooley, M., *The new technology—Social impacts and human-centred alternatives,* Technology Policy Group, Occasional Paper 4, Open University, Milton Keynes (1983).

Cooley, M., *Architect or bee?: The human price of technology,* Hogarth, London (1987).

Council for Science & Society, *New technology: Society, employment and skill—Report of a working party,* Council for Science & Society, London (1981).

Crompton, R., & G. Jones, *White-collar proletariat: Deskilling and gender in clerical work,* Macmillan, London (1984).

Downing, H., Word Processors and the oppression of women, in: T. Forrester (ed.), *The microelectronics revolution* Basil Blackwell, Oxford (1980), pp. 275–287.

Duncan, M., *Microelectronics: Five areas of subordination,* in: L. Levidow & B. Young (ed.), *Science, Technology and the Labour Process* CSE Books, London (1981).

E D P Analyzer, The experience of word processing, in: T. Forester (ed.) *The Microelectronics Revolution,* Blackwell, Oxford (1980).

European Trade Union Institute, *Negotiating technological change,* Author, Brussels (1982).

Evans, J., The worker and the workplace, in: G. Friedrichs & A. Schaff (eds.), *Microelectronics and society,* Pergamon, Oxford (1982).

Friedrichs, G., & A. Schaff (eds.), *Microelectronics and society: For better or worse. A report to the Club of Rome,* Pergamon, Oxford (1982).

Forester, T., (ed.), *The microelectronics revolution,* Blackwell, Oxford (1980).

Forester, T., (ed.), *The information technology revolution,* Blackwell, Oxford (1985).

Gennard, J., & S. Dunn, The impact of new technology on the structure and organization of craft unions in the printing industry, *British Journal of Industrial Relations,* 21(i), (1983), pp. 17–32.

Gershuny, J., *After industrial society: The emerging self-service economy,* Macmillan, London (1978).

Gill, C., *Work, unemployment, and the new technology,* Polity Press, Cambridge (1985).

Green, K., R. Coombs, & K. Holroyd, *The effects of microelectronic technologies on employment prospects: A case study of Tameside,* Gower, Farnborough (1980).

Grossman, R., Miss Micro, *New Internationalist, 150,* 1985, pp. 12–13.

Gustavsen, B., Technology and collective agreements: Some recent Scandinavian developments, *Industrial Relations Journal, 16*(3), 1985, pp. 34–42.

Hakim, C., *Employers' use of outwork,* Department of Employment Research Paper 4, Her Majesties Stationery Office, London (1985).

Handy, C., *The future of work,* Blackwell, Oxford (1984).

Hesselman, L., & R. Spellman, Responses to the employment consequences of technological change, in: D. L. Bosworth (ed.), *The employment consequences of technological change,* Macmillan, London (1983).

Hingel, A., A promethean change of industrial relations—A comparative study of Western European unions and technological developments, in: M. Warner (ed.), *Microprocessors, manpower and society,* Gower, Aldershot (1984).

Hobsbawm, E., The machine breakers, in: E. Hobsbawm (ed.), *Labouring men,* Weiderfeld & Nicholson, London (1964), pp. 5–22.

Huws, U., *Your job in the eighties: A woman's guide to new technology,* Pluto, London (1982).

Huws, U., The new home workers, *New Society* Vol. 67, No. 1113, pp. 454–455.

Ishikawa, A., Microelectronics and Japanese industrial relations, in: M. Warner (ed.), *Microprocessors, manpower and society,* Gower, Aldershot (1984), pp. 349–360.

Jacobi, O., B. Jessop, H. Kastendiek & F. M. Regini (eds.), *Technical change, rationalization and industrial relations,* Croom Helm, London (1986).

James, B., The trade union response to new technology, in: D. L. Bosworth (ed.) *The employment consequences of technological change,* Macmillan, London (1983).

Japan External Trade Organization, Industrial robots, *Now in Japan* (No. 32), 1981, Author, Tokyo (1981).

Jenkins, C., & B. Sherman, *The collapse of work*, Eyre Methuen, London (1983).

Joint Forum of Combine Committees, *The control of new technology: Trade union strategies in the workplace*, Author, London (1982).

Jones, B., *Sleepers, wake!: Technology and the future of work*, Wheatsheaf Books, Brighton (1982).

Jones, B., Destruction or redistribution of engineering skills? The case of numerical control, in: S. Wood (ed.), *The degradation of work? Skill, de-skilling and the labour process*, Hutchinson, London (1982), pp. 179–200.

Knights, D., H. Willmott & D. Collinson (eds), *Job redesign—Critical perspectives on the labor process*, Gower, Aldershot (1985).

Kondratiev, N., The long waves in economic life (reprint), *Lloyds Bank Review*, Vol. 129, (1978), pp. 41–60.

Kumar, K., *Prophecy and progress: The sociology of industrial and post-industrial society*, Penguin, Harmondsworth (1978).

Labor Research Department, *VDU's, Health and Jobs*, Author, London (1985).

Large, P., *The micro revolution revisited*, Frances Pinter, London (1984).

Lash, S., The end of neo-corporatism?: The breakdown of centralized bargaining in Sweden, *British Journal of Industrial Relations*, 23(2), 1985, pp. 215–239.

MacInnes, J., *The question of flexibility*, University of Glasgow Department of Social and Economic Research, Research Paper 5, University of Glasgow (1987).

Manwaring, T., The trade union response to new technology, *Industrial Relations Journal*, 12(4), 1981, pp. 7–25.

Martin, R., *New technology and industrial relations in Fleet Street*, in: M. Warner (ed.), *Microprocessors, Manpower and Society* Gower, Aldershot (1984).

Masuda, Y., *Computopia*, in: T. Forester (ed.) *The information technology revolution*, Blackwell, Oxford (1985), pp. 620–634.

I.G. Metall, *Der erste Schritt unserer Gegenwehr*, [extracts translated as *The first step in our fight back: First interim report of IGM convenor's committee on the rationalization of Opel in Bochum*,] Author, Bochum (1984).

Moore, R., & H. Levie, The impact of new technology on trade union organization, *Social change and technology in Europe Information Bulletin, No. 8*, Commission of the European Community, Brussels (1982).

Mumford, E., & D. Henshaw, *Participative approach to computer systems design*, Associated Business Press, London (1979).

National Computing Center & AUEW/TASS, *Computer technology and employment*, Author, Manchester (1979).

National Graphical Association, *Printing and change*, Author, Bedford (no date).

Nichols, T., & H. Beynon, *Living with capitalism*, Routledge & Kegan Paul, London (1977).

Nitta, M., Current state of the home duty work system in Japan, *Japan Labor Bulletin*, Vol. 25(2), 1986, pp. 6–8.

Noble, D., Social choice in machine design: the case of automatically controlled machine tools, in: A. Zimbalist (ed.), *Case Studies on the labor process*, Monthly Review Press, New York (1979).

Nora, S., & A. Minc, *The computerization of society—A report to the president of France*, MIT Press, London (1980).

T. Nuki, The effect of microelectronics on the Japanese style of management, *Labor & Society*, 8(4), (1983), pp. 393–400.

Organisation for Economic Cooperation and Development, *Trends in the information economy*, Committee for Information, Computer and Communications Policy, Paper 11, Author, Paris (1986).

Peitchinis, S. G., *Computer technology and employment: Retrospect and prospect*, Macmillan, London (1983).

Perlowski, A., The smart machine revolution, in: T. Forester (ed.), *The Microelectronics Revolution*, Blackwell, Oxford (1980).

Rada, J., *The impact of microelectronics*, International Labor Office, Geneva (1980).

Ramsay, H., What is participation for? in: D. Knights, H. Willmott, & D. Collinson (eds.), *Job redesign—critical perspectives on the labor process*, Gower, Aldershot (1985).

Ramsay, H., & M. Beirne, Computer redesign and "labor process" theory: Towards a critical appraisal, Department of Industrial Relations, University of Strathclyde (1986).

Rose, M., *Reworking the work ethic*, Batsford, London (1985).

Rosenbroch, H., Social and engineering design of an FMS, Paper to CAPE '83, Amsterdam (1983).

Ruskin College Trade Union Research Unit, *Seminar report: Trade unions, new technology, and the disclosure of company information*, Ruskin College, Oxford (1982).

Sherman, B., *Working at leisure*, Methuen, London (1986).

Sleigh, J., B. Boatwright, P. Irwin, & R. Stanyon, *The manpower implications of microelectronic technology, Her Majesties Stationery Office, London (1979)*.

Society of Graphical and Allied Trades '82, New technology: The American experience, Author, Hadleigh (1985).

Stonier, T., The third industrial revolution, in: T. Stonier, *Microprocessors and robots: Effects of modern technology on workers (IMF Discussion Paper)*, International Metalworkers Federation, Vienna (1979).

Stonier, T., *The wealth of information: A profile of the post-industrial society*, Methuen, London (1982).

Takagi, I., *Trade unions' responses to microelectronization in Japan*, Social and Economic Research in Modern Japan Occasional Paper 25, Free University of Berlin, Berlin (1982).

Toffler, A., *The third wave*, Bantam, London (1981).

Trades Union Congress, *Employment and technology*, Author, London (1979).

Utopia Project, *Report No. 2*, Arbetslivcentrum, Stockholm (1981).

Warner, M., (ed.), *Microprocessors, manpower, and society*, Gower, Aldershot (1984).

Werneke, D., *Microelectronics and office jobs—The impact of the chip on women's employment*, International Labor Office, Geneva (1983).

Whymant, R., The cradle to the grave system is taking a battering in Japan, *Guardian*, (August 17, 1983).

Wilkinson, B., *The shopfloor politics of new technology*, Heinemann, London (1983).

Williams, R., & F. Steward, Technology agreements in Great Britain: A survey 1977–1983 *Industrial Relations Journal*, *16*(3), 1985, pp. 58–73.

INDEX